CONTENTS

Abbreviations		2
Introduction and Acknowledgements		2
1	From Decay to Resurgence	3
2	Putin *Aktiengesellschaft*	15
3	Putin's Cannon Fodder	32
4	Last-Minute Moves	33
5	The first Week of the Three-Day Invasion	37
6	City Fortresses	45
7	Line of Control	50
8	The Race to Odesa	53

Appendices
I	Known Major Units of the Ukrainian Army, Territorial Defence & National Guard as of February 2022	62
II	Primary Combat Units of the SV/VSRF, 2014	66
III	VKS and VMF, Major Units, 2018-20221	67

Bibliography	70
Notes	71
About the Authors	76

Helion & Company Limited
Unit 8 Amherst Business Centre
Budbrooke Road
Warwick
CV34 5WE
England
Tel. 01926 499 619
Email: info@helion.co.uk
Website: www.helion.co.uk
Twitter: @helionbooks
Visit our blog http://blog.helion.co.uk/

Text © Tom Cooper, Adrien Fontanellaz, Ed Crowther and Milos Sipos 2023
Photographs © as individually credited
Colour artwork © Giorgio Albertini, David Bocquelet, Tom Cooper 2023
Maps drawn by and © Tom Cooper 2023

Designed and typeset by Farr out Publications, Wokingham, Berkshire
Cover design Paul Hewitt, Battlefield Design (www.battlefield-design.co.uk)

Every reasonable effort has been made to trace copyright holders and to obtain their permission for the use of copyright material. The author and publisher apologise for any errors or omissions in this work, and would be grateful if notified of any corrections that should be incorporated in future reprints or editions of this book.

ISBN 978-1-804512-16-6

British Library Cataloguing-in-Publication Data
A catalogue record for this book is available from the British Library

All rights reserved. No part of this publication may be reproduced, stored in a retrieval system, or transmitted, in any form, or by any means, electronic, mechanical, photocopying, recording or otherwise, without the express written consent of Helion & Company Limited.

We always welcome receiving book proposals from prospective authors.

MAP OF EUROPE SINCE 1992

Note: In order to simplify the use of this book, all names, locations and geographic designations are as provided in *The Times World Atlas*, or other traditionally accepted major sources of reference, as of the time of described events.

ABBREVIATIONS

APC	armoured personnel carrier	MRAP	mine-resistant, ambush protected (vehicle)
ATGM	anti-tank guided missile	MRLS	multiple rocket launch system
ATMS	automated tactical control system	MP	*Morskaya pekhota* (Naval Infantry [marines]) (Russia)
BMD	*Boyevaya Mashina Desanta* (airborne combat vehicle)	NATO	North Atlantic Treaty Organisation
BMP	*Boyevaya Mashina Pyekhoty* (infantry combat vehicle)	NCO	Non-Commissioned Officer
BTG	*batalonnaja takticheskaja gruppa* (battalion tactical group) (Russia and Ukraine)	ObrAA	Independent Army Aviation Brigade (Ukraine)
		OK	Operational Command (Ukraine)
BTR	*bronyetransportyor* (armoured personnel carrier)	OSK	Strategic Operational Command or Military District (Russia)
CAA	Combined Arms Army (Russia)		
Division	in addition to its common use in the West, division (or *divizion*) is used to describe an artillery or air defence battalion in Russia and Ukraine	SBU	*Sluzhba Bezpeky Ukrayiny*, Ukraine Security Service
		SIGINT	signals intelligence
		SOF	special operation forces
		SPG	self-propelled gun
DPR	Donetsk People's Republic (para-state declared by separatists in eastern Ukraine)	SV	*Sukhoputnyje voyska* (Ground troops) (Russia)
		TD/TO	Territorial Defence (Ukraine)
DshV	*Desantno-shturmovi viyska Ukrayiny* (air assault troops) (Ukraine)	UAV	Unmanned Aerial Vehicle
		UCAV	Unmanned Combat Aerial Vehicle
ELINT	electronic intelligence	UN	United Nations
EW	electronic warfare	USSR	Union of Soviet Socialist Republics (also 'Soviet Union')
FSB	*Federalnaya Sluzhba Bezopasnosti* (Federal Security Service) (Russia)		
		UTCS	Unitied Tactical Control System (Russia)
GenStab	*Generalnyi shtab* (General Staff) (Russia and Ukraine)	VDV	*Vozdushno-desantnye voyska* (airborne troops) (Russia)
GRU	*Glavnoye Razvedyatelnoye Upravleniye* (Main Intelligence Directorate) (Russia)		
		VKS	*Vozdushno-kosmicheskiye sily* (Air-Space Force) (Russia)
IADS	integrated air defence system		
IAP	International Airport	VMF	*Voyenno-morskoy flot* (Russian Navy)
IFV	infantry fighting vehicle	VSRF	*Vooruzhonnije Síly Rossíyskoj Federátsii* (Armed Forces of the Russian Federation)
LPR	Luhansk People's Republic (para-state declared by separatists in north-eastern Ukraine)		
		VVS	*Voyenno-vozdushnye sily Rossii* (Russian Air Force, a branch of the VKS from 2015)
LOC	Line of Control		
MANPAD	man portable air defence (system)		
MBT	main battle tank	ZSU	*Zbroini syly Ukrainy* (Armed Forces of Ukraine)

INTRODUCTION AND ACKNOWLEDGEMENTS

Sparked by the aggression of the Russian Federation in February 2014, the War in Ukraine – also known as the 'Russo-Ukrainian War', or the 'Russian Invasion of Ukraine' – is probably the most-publicised armed conflict in the history of humankind. Thousands of articles and numerous books have been published since its outbreak, especially since the Russian invasion of Ukraine in February 2022. It thus might appear as if there is little or no need for an additional publication, or even this introduction. However, on the military level, this conflict is influenced by a labyrinthine 'system of systems': countless factors influencing the military capabilities and intentions of both of the involved parties, and their allies abroad.

The aim of this book, the second in a sub-series on the War in Ukraine of Helion's Europe@War series is to discern hard facts from the massive propaganda campaigns and sea of hear-say emitted by almost all of the involved parties, plus much background noise. Obviously, in the case of an ongoing conflict, this is a particularly tough task: all too many details about specific factors, personalities, units, campaigns and battles of this war remain unknown, and are going to remain unknown for a while longer. Nevertheless, the @War team has decided to try to provide a book that might become useful for additional research in the future: one providing a review of information about the involved forces, their capabilities and intentions, and their operations during the first few weeks of the war, as available over a period of three to 10 months after the invasion of February 2022. The result is anything but the *only* truth: research upon topics of this kind never ends, and thus we not only intend to pursue our related work in the form of additional similar books but hope that this one might inspire – perhaps even 'provoke' – additional research elsewhere.

1
FROM DECAY TO RESURGENCE

In late February 2022, the Armed Forces of Ukraine (*Zbroini syly Ukrainy*, ZSU), surprised the entire world by mounting effective resistance to its mighty Russian counterpart. However, what was often overlooked was the immense amount of funding and sheer energy the country invested into rebuilding its military in the aftermath of the 2014 debacle.

From Giant to Dwarf
On 24 August 1991, the Supreme Soviet of the Ukrainian Soviet Socialist Republic – then still a part of the Union of Soviet Socialist Republics (USSR, colloquially 'Soviet Union') – issued the Act of Declaration of Independence of Ukraine. Taking place only two days after the failure of a coup d'état in Moscow run by hardliners of the Communist Party of the Soviet Union and top ranks of the Soviet armed forces, and at the same time nearly all the other 15 Soviet Republics declared their independence, this act signalled the beginning of the end of the USSR, the political and economic system of which proved irreformable. Five months later, on 25 December 1991, the last General Secretary of the Soviet Union, Mikhail Gorbachev, officially declared the Soviet Union to be dissolved, with effect from the following day.

Until that point in time, the Soviet armed forces had maintained a massive presence in Ukraine: indeed, the Carpathian, Kiev, and Odessa Military Districts: a total of five armies and one army corps, with 21 divisions, 6,500 main battle tanks (MBTs) and 7,000 other armoured fighting vehicles – were all part of the second strategic echelon, the primary purpose of which was to reinforce the first echelon in the event of a major military conflict with powers of the North Atlantic Treaty Organisation (NATO) in Central or Eastern Europe. Of course, Kiev – or *Kyiv* in Ukrainian – had no need of such a massive army and was hopelessly out of condition to sustain it. Unsurprisingly, the Armed Forces of Ukraine spent the following two decades in an almost continuous process of downsizing and reducing. By 2013, only a shadow of the former three Soviet military districts and its 21 divisions remained – primarily in the form of giant 'tank graveyards', full of disused armoured fighting vehicles. Under agreements reached with the Organisation for Security and Co-operation in Europe (OSCE), the ground forces component of the ZSU was reduced to two tank brigades (1st and 17th), seven mechanised brigades (24th, 28th, 30th, 51st, 72nd, 92nd and 93rd), four airborne (or airmobile) brigades (25th, 79th, 80th, and 95th), two artillery brigades (26th and 55th), and one mountain brigade (128th). The special operation forces (SOF) component, was reduced to two regiments (3rd and 8th), and there were three artillery and/or artillery rocket regiments (15th, 27th, and 107th), and the 39th Air Defence Regiment, as well as a miscellany of independent battalions, foremost of which were two for reconnaissance purposes (54th and 74th), and two of Naval Infantry (1st and 501st). As of 2013, these forces were subjected to the control of two Operational Commands: North and South, and the VIII Army Corps. Ironically, most of the units were still home-based in western Ukraine, in the same bases constructed during Soviet times, and positioned suitably for their rapid redeployment in the direction of central and western Europe. Overall strength of the ZSU decreased significantly: from 466,000 in 1996, to 214,850 in 2012 (including about 45,000 civilian personnel), as did its budget, from 2.8 percent of the GDP in 1997, to slightly less than 1 percent in 2013. To say that this resulted in plummeting readiness rates, non-existent training standards, next to no periodic maintenance of available equipment, and no acquisition of new weapons systems – would be an understatement, because the situation was much worse. Before long, corruption – already endemic within the political and economic system of the country – spread into the armed forces too: draft dodging became endemic, and numerous military bases fell into decay. Even so, this was not yet to be the lowest ebb of the ZSU. Still considered much too big to be sustainable, it was subjected to further budget cuts. Conscription was abolished from the end of 2013, and in early 2014, Kyiv announced its intention to disband the 17th Tank Brigade. By that time, the virtually only military operation still undertaken with any measure of success was the involvement of numerous battalion-sized detachments with different peacekeeping missions of the United Nations (UN), and occasional joint exercises with NATO.

Above all of this – and especially during the administration of President Viktor Fedorovych Yanukovych, from 2010 until 2014 – the indoctrination of the ZSU was that an armed conflict with the Russian Federation was unthinkable. Moreover, Yanukovich promulgated additional budget cuts and a downsizing of the total manpower to 120,900. Overall, the armed forces were well on the way to being converted into an undertrained and underfunded midget, barely sufficient to counter internal unrest.

Maidan Uprising and Consequences
In November 2013, a wave of demonstrations and civil unrest spread over Ukraine. Sparked by the sudden decision of Yanukovich's government not to sign an association agreement with the European Union (despite an overwhelming parliamentary decision to do so), but to establish closer ties to the Russian Federation instead, protests then began opposing widespread government corruption and the influence of oligarchy, abuse of power, and violation of human rights. When the authorities attempted to violently disperse demonstrators, on 30 November 2013, the situation escalated to a near civil war. Despite draconian anti-protest laws, demonstrations intensified through early 2014, culminating in a series of street clashes in Kyiv on 19–22 January. A month later, outright street battles erupted between Maidan activists (named after the *Maidan Nezalezhnosti* – Independence Square – in Kyiv) and police, resulting in over 110 deaths. Although signing an agreement about the creation of an interim government, on 21 February 2014, the writing was now on the wall for the Yanukovich administration. He fled the country, and was then officially removed from office.

Tsar of Corruption
Yanukovich's downfall was a 'red line' for the President of the Russian Federation, Vladimir Vladimirovich Putin. Putin was an autocrat established in power in Moscow in 1999 because – as a former officer of the Committee for State Security of the USSR (*Komitet Gosudarstvennoy Bezopasnosti*, KGB), and then a director of the Federal Security Service of the Russian Federation (*Federalnaya sluzhba bezopasnosti*, FSB) – he was the sole person in a position to guarantee unaccountability of the deeply corrupt, ailing President

Boris Nikolayevich Yeltsin. To improve his public standing through a demonstration of power, in August 1999 Putin provoked the Second Chechen War through a series of false-flag bombings staged by the FSB, in which over 300 Russian civilians were killed in cold blood. During the second half of 1999, the Armed Forces of the Russian Federation (*Vooruzhonnije Síly Rossíyskoj Federátsii*, VSRF) invaded Chechnya, completely demolished and then conquered its capital of Grozny, and, starting in May 2000, established a pro-Moscow regime. Although the large-scale armed resistance by Chechens went on for nine years longer, Putin thus achieved his first military victory which secured him a win in the presidential elections held in March 2000.

Over the following years, Putin's sole political program became the security of his own rule: nominally elected in democratic elections, he ruled with the help of a rapidly growing propaganda machinery that cultivated a cult of personality of him as macho, a tough superhero, and a genius strategist, while building up a system of corruption and patronage vastly superior to any kind of organised crime, and making extensive use of force and repression to silence any kind of serious political opposition. While enriching himself and his supporters thanks to massive increase in the price of oil and gas, and numerous major oil and gas export deals concluded with the West, he initiated a reform of the VSRF in 2006, invaded Georgia in 2008, and began providing support to dictatorships in the Russian neighbourhood and beyond. Unsurprisingly, Putin gradually developed strong antagonism vis-à-vis pluralism, and began considering democracy to be the primary threat to his regime: he began fearing opposition to his – and to any other – dictatorship. Nowhere was this fear as obvious as in the case of Ukraine, which he repeatedly failed to subjugate through supporting 'pro-Russian politicians.'

The Coup in Sevastopol

As soon as Yanukovich fled to Russia, during the night of 22 to 23 February 2014, Putin convened a meeting of all chiefs of his security services, and issued a directive to 'return Crimea to Russia'. Only four days later, pro-Russian demonstrations were staged in Sevastopol, while masked Russian troops wearing no insignia – colloquially known as the 'Little Green Men' – captured all strategic sites over the peninsula. In a rapid sequence of events, a pro-Russian government was established, which quickly declared independence from Ukraine on 16 March 2014 and – only two days later – the peninsula was formally annexed by Russia.

Because the annexation of the Crimean Peninsula was enacted by the Armed Forces of the Russian Federation, this was an aggression, an invasion, and thus a blatant violation of international law and territorial integrity of Ukraine; a violation of the 1975 Helsinki Accords; a violation of the 1994 Budapest Memorandum on Security Assurances, and the 1997 Treaty on Friendship, Cooperation, and Partnership between Moscow and Kyiv. Unsurprisingly, Putin's action – misdescribed as 'based on the principle of self-determination of peoples', and as an action against a 'new country with which Russia had not concluded any treaties' – was met with fierce critique and condemnation by Kyiv.[1] However, at home in Russia, another successful military action served to increase Putin's popularity right at a time when the country began to suffer economic stagnation caused by his corrupt system of rule. Atop of this, the West reacted with only lukewarm condemnations and economic sanctions: while the latter sufficed to cause additional damage to the Russian economy, it soon proved too porous and too little to have the desired effects. On the contrary, starting from early 2015, first the Austrian government and then several others did their best to breach the international isolation into which Putin had manoeuvred his regime: the businesses of importing Putin's gas and oil, and exporting cars and other commodities to the Russian Federation, were much too profitable for the Western oligarchy, than to be abandoned 'just for Ukraine'.

Russo-Ukrainian War

Considering the above-mentioned, it is unsurprising that the ZSU was caught entirely unprepared by the Russian invasion of Crimea – and ill-prepared to face multiple dramas that were to follow through 2014, and which, with hindsight, are considered the beginning of the Russo-Ukrainian War, ongoing ever since.

Still seething with rage, but cautious not to provoke the West, Putin made his next move in March 2014, when a Russia-instigated armed insurrection erupted in the Donbass area in eastern Ukraine, which by mid-April had escalated into an armed uprising. Within days, chaos reigned even at the top of the state, further adding to the misery, as key figures – including the Minister of Defence and the Director of the Security Service of Ukraine (*Sluzhby bezpeky Ukrayiny*, SBU) – both fled to Russia. They were followed by a number of other key figures, including the Chief of the General Staff of the Armed Forces and the Commander of the Naval Forces. By 11 March 2014, the new Minister of Defence admitted that out of 49,100 service personnel, only 6,000 were available for immediate deployment, and that the inventory of operational equipment totalled just 236 MBTs (out of 683 that were available), 650 infantry fighting vehicles and armoured personnel carriers, 131 self-propelled guns, and 105 multiple rocket launchers. In the best case, this meant that each of the ZSU's brigades could dispatch a single Battalion Tactical Group (BTG) to the conflict zone. In reality, the situation was often much worse. For example, when ordered into Donbass, the 24th Mechanised Brigade sent its 1st Mechanised Battalion including just four 2S3 Akatsiya self-propelled howitzers, six BM-21 multiple rocket launcher systems (MRLS), a battery of 120mm mortars, a company of 10 T-64 MBTs, a reconnaissance company and a few incomplete support units. In urgency, the Parliament then pushed through a law about a partial mobilisation: however, this failed to provide decisive results because the infrastructure for the draft of men had already been disestablished following the end of compulsory service.

Nightmares of 2014

Instead of joining the ZSU, thousands of Ukrainians found themselves with little choice but to form a wide array of volunteer units. Some came into being on the initiative of the locals (see the Donbass Battalion); others were formed by political parties (Aidar, Azov and Sich battalions), while a few others were established with the help of the authorities, resulting in the so-called Territorial Defence (Dnipro-2 Battalion). Obviously, the combat efficiency and equipment of such, 'self-created' units varied immensely – though in this way it actually provided a mirror image of what was going on in the territories claimed by the self-declared Luhansk People's Republic (LPR) and the Donetsk People's Republic (DPR). Nevertheless, it was with this mix of regular armed forces operating as task forces, and volunteer units that the Ukrainians managed to defeat the Separatists in the east: by late August 2014, they significantly reduced the Separatist-controlled territory and were close to reaching the border with Russia – only to see their progress reversed by a full-fledged Russian invasion.[2]

Artillery units of the VRSF had already begun to provide fire-support to the Separatists from late July 2014: on 22 August, amid intensified shelling of the advancing Ukrainians, the first BTGs of the Russian Army crossed the border, launching a direct military intervention in what was now an undeclared war. Using the 'People's Militias' of the LPR and the DPR both as a cover to hide their involvement and as expendable light infantry, the far better equipped and trained, and numerically superior Russians quickly threw the Ukrainians back. In a series of fierce battles – like the one for Donetsk International Airport (IAP) – they pushed all the way to Debaltseve before the frontlines stabilised. Although Russia attempted to hide its involvement, it was very obvious by the time the first phase of the conflict ended with the Minsk Protocol, on 5 September 2014, signed by Ukraine, Russia, LPR and the DPR. Putin exploited the resulting situation to install his favourites in both the LPR and the DPR but abstained from repeating the exercise of the Crimea annexation – apparently because by this time his forces, and those of his proxies, had managed to capture only about 50 percent of the Luhansk and Donetsk oblasts. Following a series of ceasefire violations, in early 2015 the Minsk II agreements were signed by Russia and Ukraine, but a number of disputes prevented these from ever being fully implemented: indeed, the second treaty merely froze the 450-kilometre-long frontlines – the so-called 'Line of Control' (LOC) – and limited exchanges of fire to repeated artillery barrages and minor infantry probes against enemy positions. By that point in time, losses were already heavy: the ZSU had 2,636 killed and 8,897 wounded in the Donbass, and had to write-off over 800 armoured fighting vehicles by April 2016. The losses of the Russians and the Separatist formations remain unknown.[3]

Rebuilding the Ground Forces – on a Budget

To say that the Crimean debacle and a series of defeats in the Donbass during the second half of 2014 and early 2015 shocked the entire Ukrainian defence establishment – if not the entire nation – would be an understatement. All of a sudden, Ukraine had to expand, reorganise, and improve its armed forces, and urgently so. While not appearing anywhere on the agenda for 23 years, the ZSU suddenly became the top priority of successive governments and this was nowhere more obvious than the rapidly increasing defence budget: from US$1.9 billion in 2013, to US$3.02 billion in 2018. Even then, and as massive as this increase might appear at the first glance, it was still far from enough to enable an unimpaired build-up. The army had to be developed 'on a budget'.[4]

Table 1: Ukrainian Military Spending, 2013–2020

Year	% of GDP (MoD)	% of GDP (World Bank)
2013	0.97	1.58
2014	1.78	2.24
2015	2.53	3.25
2016	2.63	3.15
2017	2.43	2.88
2018	N/A	3.19
2019	N/A	3.5
2020	2.7	4.1

Increased budget allocations enabled the ZSU to expand the army from 165,500 (plus 44,500 civilian service men and women) in 2014, to 204,000 (and 46,000 civilians) in 2015. While the strength of the force remained the same for the next several years, by 2016 all the military personnel were contracted professionals. Nevertheless, conscription was reinstated as well, and through 2015 a total of 138 recruitment offices were operational. Meanwhile, the bulk of Territorial Defence units – and several volunteer units – created in the chaos of 2014 – was gradually integrated into the army in the form of motorised infantry battalions, and attached to existing manoeuvre brigades. Furthermore, before the end of 2015, the Army dissolved its VIII Corps and instead established four Operational Commands (OKs): North, East, South, and West. Atop of this, another corps-level formation came into being as a separate command: the High Mobility Assault Forces (renamed the Airborne Assault Troops in 2017), and the Special Forces Command was established. Meanwhile, 15 manoeuvre brigades were either newly established or reactivated and redeployed in the east and, in 2016, the Territorial Defence resuscitated. Finally, a Reserve Corps was created, including numerous reserve tank, motorised infantry, and artillery brigades, meant to build-up a strategic reserve activated in the event of war.

Table 2: Build-up of ZSU Land Forces, 2014–2018

Period	Units activated
2014	14th, 53rd and 54th Mechanised, 57th and 59th Motorised, 81st Air Assault
2015	56th and 58th Motorised, 10th Mountain Assault, 61st Jaeger
2016–2018	45th and 46th Air Assault, 35th and 36th Naval Infantry. Reserve: 3rd, 4th, 5th Tank, 60th, 62nd, 63rd, 66th Mechanised

Qualitive Edge

The Ukrainian build-up was not only quantitative in nature, but qualitative too. The Ukrainians thoroughly reviewed their 2014–2015 experience in order to identify their main shortcomings and address them as fast as they could. In turn, this led to a series of wide-ranging reforms in the army. Combat brigades and battalions were thus reshuffled to increase their firepower, noticeably by reinforcing their artillery group, with an emphasis on their anti-tank arsenal, their flexibility, and logistical capabilities.[5]

Still predominant at the time, the Soviet military doctrine was gradually abandoned and replaced by a mix of combat experiences and Russian and NATO practices.[6] For example: headquarters up to the level of brigade were all reorganised along NATO lines, and the training of the officer corps focused drastically on the *Auftragstaktik* – enabling junior officers to act as they saw fit, on the spot, always in the interest of fulfilling the mission, and without first requesting approval from superior commanders. Vast efforts were invested into building up and empowering an urgently needed corps of non-commissioned officers (NCOs) and their training along similar lines.

Finally, Ukrainians took care to introduce as many new technologies as possible, including the deployment of mini-unmanned aerial vehicles (UAVs), and to improve the communication infrastructure of the ZSO – and this both at tactical and strategic level: indeed, starting in 2015, a small team of the Central Intelligence Agency (CIA) supervised the development of techniques and technology to counter the vastly superior Russian capabilities in regards of communications intelligence (COMINT), electronic intelligence (ELINT), and signals intelligence (SIGINT)

– which, in 2014–2015 enabled the Russians to rapidly detect Ukrainian units and plaster their positions with artillery. Finally, the Ukrainians routinely rotated their special forces operators through conventional units, to pass on their knowledge, and greatly increased the number of snipers assigned to all of their units, and honed their tactics with an emphasis on targeting enemy officers.

Training of the ZSU since 2015 experienced a dramatic improvement. While as of 2014, new recruits received just three weeks of elementary training and battalion-level exercises were a rarity, basic training was stretched to two months and the number of exercises skyrocketed, as described in Table 3. In this regard, it was the support of NATO that proved instrumental: from 2014 onwards, numerous instructors from various member countries routinely served in Ukraine. A NATO training support group was established under a US-funded and led Joint Multinational Training Group-Ukraine (JMTG-U), to coordinate activities of hundreds of British, Canadian, Lithuanian, Polish, and US instructors rotated through Ukraine. This body alone managed to train about 10,000 Ukrainian servicemen a year. The primary facility related to the JMTG-U became the Yavoriv Combined Army Training Centre, located near the Polish border and fully equipped with Multiple Integrated Laser Engagement System (MILES): at least five Ukrainian battalions underwent the 55-day training curriculum there each year since 2015. In other cases, Ukrainian army units took part in multinational exercises, like Sea Breeze and Rapid Trident, while their skills were further enhanced through frequent and regular rotation in and out of the positions along the LOC, where they obtained plentiful first-hand combat experience in the course of relentless violations of the ceasefire agreement.[7]

Table 3: ZSU, Ground Unit Exercises, 2013–2017[8]

Year	Brigade-level	Battalion-level
2013	0	7
2014	0	18
2015	15	94
2016	20	125
2017	35	168

Operational Reserves 1 and 2

Of crucial importance for the overhaul of the land component of the ZSU was a complete reconstitution and reform, and the establishment of the Operational Reserve System. Starting in 2016, this aimed to bring both active and reserve units to full strength in the event of war. The importance of the Operational Reserve System cannot be overemphasised, because budget constraints dictated that the majority of active brigades to be kept at just 30–60 percent of their nominal strength, while brigades of the Reserve Corps were mostly at only 10 percent: correspondingly, both types of formations needed massive reinforcements by reservists before engaging in high-intensity combat operations.

Including 230,000 reservists, in 2020 the Operational Reserve System was divided into two classes: the Operational Reserve 1 (OR-1), tasked with completing the effectiveness of the active and reserve combat units in the event of mobilisation; and the Operational Reserve-2 (OR-2), where reservists were assigned to second-line units of the Army, or of the Territorial Defence. All reservists assigned to the OR-1 and OR-2 were recalled to refresh their training – usually in their parent brigades – at least once every two years, and in grand total, 41,000 troops served with the OR-1 and 66,000 with OR-2 between 2017 and 2020. In this fashion, the ZSU built-up a strong body of reservists, who remained current in their military functions, and whose parent brigades were capable of rapidly switching to intensive combat operations.[9]

A row of overhauled and upgraded T-64s in the process of being handed over to the ZSU. (Ukrainian MOD)

Rearming by Overhauling

Obviously, such a massive amount of active and reservist troops required an appropriate amount of equipment – even more so because of the losses sustained in Donbas, and the limited defence budget. This is where the major factories, an entire complex of workshops, and the research and development enterprises that Ukraine inherited from the USSR came in handy. Indeed, as in the case of the ZSU, this sector was totally oversized for the needs upon independence, yet starved of significant orders from the government and foreign customers over the following 20 years. While up to 90 percent of the companies in question eventually had to cease operating in the 1990s, those that survived did so thanks to orders from abroad. Amongst the most significant commercial deals was a Pakistani order for 320 T-80UD tanks, which provided at least some respite. However, the majority of such deals were related to small scale sales of overhauled surplus equipment inherited from the Soviet armed forces, for example to Chad, Northern Macedonia, or a few other customers in Africa. Research, development and production of new equipment remained limited to such designs as the BTR-3 APC, T-64 Bulat and T-80 Oplot MBTs, and R-77 medium range, active-radar homing, air-to-air missiles. Unsurprisingly, one local expert concluded: 'Since the collapse of the Soviet Union, for 30 long years, Ukraine has ceased to be a country developing modern weapons.'[10]

As of 2010, what was left of the defence sector was brought under the control of the state-owned corporation Ukroboronprom. Even then, the defence industries experienced another setback in 2014: at the time, most of it was still intensively cooperating with Russia, but then all ties were cut off. Certainly enough, the resulting damage was severe for both sides: Russia lost its source of a number of key components for most of its advanced and heavy weaponry, while Ukroboronprom lost its primary customers. Nevertheless, during the following eight years of 'no-peace, no war' the capability of the Ukrainian defence sector to not only overhaul and modernise, but also to manufacture new equipment – ranging from mortars and artillery pieces to armoured vehicles, missiles and combat aircraft – was to prove of crucial importance.

Indeed, from 2014 onwards, dozens of newly produced systems were acquired by the ZSU, including as many as 500 T-64BV Model 2017, T-72AMT, and T-84 MBTs, 200 BTR-4, BMP-1TS and BMP-1U APCs, and several types of mine-resistant, ambush protected vehicles (MRAPs). Furthermore, Ukroboronprom – which as of 2017–2021 included 107 companies employing 67,000 people – launched licence production of Israeli-designed Tavor assault rifles, several types of highly potent anti-tank guided missiles (ATGMs; such as the RK-3 Corsar and Stugna-P), and the local variant of the Krasnopol guided 152mm artillery shell, named Kvitnyk. Atop of this, a large number of older armoured vehicles, artillery pieces, and anti-aircraft systems were recovered from rusting in 'open storage' around the country, refurbished and returned to service – many of them by small enterprises and workshops operated by the ZSU – enabling Ukraine to bolster its armed forces at a relatively low cost. The price to pay was that much of the equipment was dated – a factor even more important because several modernisation programs failed, while the development of other new weapons systems was abandoned due to the lack of funding. In yet other cases, money was squandered through endemic corruption. In particular, the ZSU was vexed by the lack of facilities for production and storage of heavy artillery ammunition. This became a crucial issue because of a series of 'mysterious incidents' in several ammunition depots starting in 2014, which destroyed up to 210,000 tons of 122mm artillery rockets and 152mm shells, causing acute shortages of both – which could not be solved even through urgent orders for replacements from companies in Bulgaria and the Czech Republic.[11]

Defensive Weapons

The war of 2014 triggered constantly intensifying cooperation between Ukraine and several members of NATO – primarily in the form of training, but also in terms of arms acquisitions. The USA provided the bulk of the latter (worth US$2.7 billion between 2014 and 2017). Concerns of antagonising the Russians resulted in much of the NATO-supplied equipment being of 'non-lethal' nature: however, some was critical – especially in regards of communication, night vision equipment, and first-aid kids. Body armour – well-fitting to new, NATO-like uniforms with digital camouflage patterns, introduced by the ZSU – a shipment of 230 High Mobility Multipurpose Wheeled Vehicles (HMMWV, colloquially 'Humvee'), and a few patrol boats were appreciated by Ukrainians. Weaponry began arriving only in late 2017, and then in the form of defensive systems, including 39 launchers and 210 FGM-148 Javelin medium anti-armour weapon systems, followed by 10 additional launchers

Since 2014, the Ukrainian truck maker KrAZ has carried out licence production of the Canadian-designed STREIT Group Spartan armoured personnel carrier. (Ukrainian MOD)

A Ukrainian BM-30 Uragan system seen during a fire action. (Ukrainian MOD)

and 150 missiles, and several shipments of light firearms and related ammunition in 2019. The last known pre-war shipment of 30 Javelin launchers and 180 missiles arrived only in 2021. Apart from the USA, a few other countries donated military equipment – mainly with the aim of helping to bring the ZSU up to NATO standards. For example, Great Britain donated 75 surplus Saxon APCs, Canada 39 STREIT Group Spartan APCs, Poland provided 54 old MT-LB APCs and 83 BMP-1 infantry fighting vehicles (IFVs), and the Czech Republic donated 49 2S1 Gvozdika 122mm self-propelled howitzers.

It was only amid the growing crisis in mid-2021 that there was a marked change in NATO's behaviour: by the end of that year, and through early 2022, the influx of Western armament into Ukraine increased dramatically. The US shipped a total of 300 Javelin missiles in several batches, followed by 75 AeroVironment RQ-11 Raven UAVs; Great Britain followed with 2,000 of its own Next Generation Light Anti-Tank Weapon (NLAW); Lithuania provided additional Javelins and – together with Latvia – sent a batch of FIM-92 Stinger MANPADS; Poland supplied locally manufactured Grom MANPADs (further development of the 9K38 Igla, codenamed 'SA-24 Grinch' by the ASCC/NATO). However, the acquisition that was to prove most important for the first phase of the war took place in 2019, when Kyiv and Ankara signed a contract worth US$69 million for the purchase of 12 Bayraktar TB.2 unmanned combat aerial vehicles (UCAVs) together with MAM mini-precision guided munitions. This agreement also subsequently led to the decision to launch the production of TB.2s under licence in Ukraine.[12]

Ground Forces of the ZSU as of February 2022

As of 2022, the organisation of the ZSU began with its supreme command and control body, the General Staff (GenStab-U), whose functions had now been reorganised along NATO lines. Correspondingly, it included the posts of J-2: intelligence, and J-3: operations.

In turn, the GenStab controlled the main branches of the armed forces, including the Air Force, Land Forces, and Naval Forces, Airborne Assault Troops, Special Operation Forces, and the Joint Forces Command – which was in charge of operations along the LOC in Luhansk and Donbas. The next level of commands reported directly to the GenStab-U, and included the Support Forces, Logistic Forces, Signal and Cyber Security Troops, and Medical Forces.

As of February 2022, the Land Forces included a total of 18 active brigades (of which two were tank, nine mechanised, four motorised, two mountain assault and one jaeger), eight artillery, missile, or rocket artillery brigades, and four anti-aircraft missile regiments (the latter all equipped with Osa-AKM systems). In peacetime, all these units were staffed at 30–60 percent of their wartime effectives, but also with up to 90 percent of their equipment.

One of the four artillery brigades was assigned to each of four OKs (North, East, South and West). In addition to artillery brigades, and depending on need, each OK further controlled a number of manoeuvre brigades, one anti-aircraft missile regiment, and other specialised units, such as a reconnaissance battalion and a signals regiment. Moreover, the OKs were in operational control over all brigades of the Territorial Defence active within their areas of responsibility. Three additional tank, three mechanised, a motorised, and two artillery brigades of the Reserve Corps were staffed at between 5 and 10 percent of their nominal strength, but most were lacking heavy weaponry – even though now re-equipped with T-72s donated by NATO members.

Most of the firepower of the Land Forces was contained within the artillery, rocket artillery, and missile brigades, each of which included three or four divisions. The sole missile brigade was entirely equipped with overhauled OTR-21 Tochka tactical ballistic missiles (ASCC/NATO-codename 'SS-21 Scarab'), and the sole rocket artillery brigade with BM-27 Uragan multiple rocket launchers. Two independent artillery regiments were both equipped with BM-30 Smerch MRLSs. The four artillery brigades operated mostly self-propelled howitzers such as the 2S5 Giatsint-S, 2S7 Pion, and 2S19 Msta, but also a number of towed artillery pieces, like the 2A36 Giatsint-B and 2A65 Msta-B. All of these were of 152mm, except for the Pions, which were 203mm calibre. Each artillery brigade further included a reconnaissance battalion, one anti-tank division (equipped with MT-12 Rapirs), and a motorised infantry battalion – in addition to the usual support companies.

A platoon of T-64BM Bulat tanks of the ZSU on an exercise in the late 2010s. (Ukrainian MOD)

An MT-LB armoured personnel carrier, carrying a ZU-23-2 anti-aircraft gun on its rear deck, and a similar ZU-23-2 gun on the ground, both belonging to an airborne assault unit of the ZSU, seen during a pre-war exercise. (Ukrainian MOD)

Nominally at least, each tank brigade of the ZSU had three tank battalions and a mechanised battalion, each with a total of 41 MBTs (13 per company), 30–40 IFVs, and 500 troops. A mechanised brigade included three mechanised battalions and one tank battalion, with a total of about 40 IFVs and 31 MBTs. Both tank and mechanised brigades included an artillery group of four divisions (one with 18 2S1s, one with 18 2S3 Akatsiya, and another with 18 BM-21 Grad MRLS), and an anti-tank division equipped with 12 MT-12 Rapira towed anti-tank guns and nine Shturm-S tank destroyers. The air defence division of each tank or mechanised brigade nominally included six 2S6 Tunguska self-propelled anti-aircraft guns, and 8–12 Strela-10 self-propelled SAMs. Their supporting elements included companies of engineers, maintenance and logistics, reconnaissance, snipers, electronic warfare (EW), and medics. Overall, Ukrainian tank and mechanised brigades were thus very similar to their nominal Russian counterparts – both in organisation and firepower:

KROPYVA: THE UKRAINIAN ARTILLERY APP

The Russian and Ukrainian armies of the early 2020s were both born out of the defunct Soviet army and retained many similarities. One of the most salient was the predominant role played by artillery, Stalin's beloved 'God of War'. From mid-2014 to early 2015, Russian and Ukrainian troops clashed in the Donbass, and the latter suffered several severe defeats. One of the keys to Russia's early successes was the superiority of its 'fire-reconnaissance complex': the combination of reconnaissance drones, electronic warfare and communications equipment and artillery batteries. This complex allowed the Russians to drown the enemy in a deluge of fire within 15 minutes of their detection. Eighty percent of Ukrainian losses during the period were caused by Russian artillery as a result.

The Ukrainian army was in a sorry state after years of insufficient funding and had to be reconstituted in a hurry, to the point where the Ministry of Defence was ready to accept the support of various patriotic associations. One of them, Army SOS, enquired about the needs of the military and within a few months developed *Kropyva* (Urtica or nettles), a mapping intelligence application running on Android that allows a person with a terminal, usually a tablet, to easily mark an enemy position. The software then transmits the indication to nearby artillery pieces while allowing the coordination of their fire, resulting in synchronised fire against the same target from several separate positions. Communication between the system elements is maintained by satellite transmission. While in military parlance such a system is defined as an Automatic Tactical Management System (ATMS), *Kropyva* functions as a form of Uber for artillery and has made it possible to drastically increase its reaction time while reducing its vulnerability. The average time required to deploy a howitzer battery has been reduced by a factor of 5 — to three minutes; the time required to engage a non-pre-planned target by a factor of 3, to one minute; while the time required to open counterbattery fire has been divided by 10, down to 30 seconds. In a nutshell, combined with the systematic use of drones for fire correction, *Kropyva* has increased the effectiveness of Ukrainian artillery by an order of magnitude, acting as a force multiplier.

The application has since been further developed through close cooperation between users and developers, with the flexibility and versatility of the system increasing over time. It can now be used for de-mining tasks too. As a result of this agile approach, the use of associations or small companies and the abundance of local IT specialists, the Ukrainians were able to develop a system quickly and at very low cost. It is also considered to be better than those in use in the US armed forces today thanks to its flexibility, while other Western armies still can only dream about such capabilities.

The Russians identified the threat embodied by *Kropyva* years before 2022. The hacker group Fancy Bear reportedly targeted the application between 2014 and 2016, but without apparent or sustained success. At the start of the hostilities in late February 2022, Russian cyber units mainly launched a systematic attack on Ukrainian satellite connection terminals to disrupt their communications at the strategic and operational level, and thus *Kropyva* largely remained operational. Kyiv responded by introducing Starlink, a satellite communications network set up by SpaceX. Since then, Elon Musk's company has proved itself to be expert in neutralising Russian cyber and jamming attacks, ensuring, among other things, that *Kropyva* remained up and running throughout 2022, and was subsequently supplanted by a much more secure ATMS.[14]

Forward artillery observer of the ZSU, with the Kropyva terminal. (Army SOS)

Terminal of the Kropyva ATMS. (Army SOS)

indeed, like the Russians, the Ukrainians were trained to operate in the form of highly flexible battalion tactical groups (BTGs), each of which usually consisted of one tank and three mechanised companies, supported by an artillery battery, and other support elements as necessary. However, it seems that as of February 2022, each Ukrainian tank and mechanised brigade was reinforced by an additional battalion of motorised infantry, and other elements. For example, the 92nd Mechanised Brigade ('Mech') is known to have included two tank, two mechanised and one motorised battalions.

Ukrainian motorised brigades were much lighter formations, better suited for mobile defence, but lacking heavy armament. All of them consisted of three motorised battalions (each supported by one tank company); an artillery group (including a division of three batteries with six D-30 towed howitzers each), and one division of BM-21 MRLS (each with one or two batteries of six launchers each); an anti-tank division (equipped with MT-12s only), an anti-aircraft division (Strela-10s and ZU-23 towed anti-aircraft guns), and support units in the form of reconnaissance, engineer, maintenance, logistics, medical and sniper companies.

The two Mountain Assault Brigades possessed slightly more firepower and stronger support elements than motorised infantry brigades (including a full tank battalion), but were less powerful than mechanised formations, while the single jaeger brigade was equipped and trained for operations in the marshy terrain of northern central Ukraine.

The Command of Airborne Assault Troops of the ZSU (*Desantno-shturmovi viyska Ukrayiny*, DshV) controlled another seven brigades (one airborne and six air assault), the equipment and training of which can be described as 'shock light infantry'. Each consisted of three airborne assault battalions, supported by one tank battalion (equipped with T-80 MBTs), one artillery group (two batteries of D-30s or 2S1 Gvozdikas and one of BM-21s), one anti-aircraft and one engineer battalion, and companies for landing support, maintenance, logistics, medical- and other support-related purposes. While the 25th Airborne was equipped with purpose-designed BMD-1 and BMD-2 light IFVs, the other units of this type operated a miscellany of BTR-70, BTR-80, BTR-3, BTR-4, MT-LB and Spartan APCs and IFVs.

The Navy added two Naval Infantry brigades – the 35th and 36th – to the total, both of which were, essentially, motorised infantry formations with support elements of a mechanised brigade (including a tank battalion). Moreover, the naval forces included the 37th Artillery Brigade with one division of BM-27s and two of BM-21s. Finally, the Special Operations Command – which comprised units drawn from both the Land Forces and the Navy – included the 3rd and 8th Special Operations Forces Regiments, the 73rd Maritime SOF Centre, 140th Special Purpose Centre, and 801st Anti-Diversionary Detachment, together with four operation-centres (one for each OKs). The Special Operations Command exercised administrative control over the 61st Jaeger Brigade: this unit, specially trained for operations in dense forests and marshes along the border with Belarus, included three motorised infantry battalions, one tank battalion, an artillery group (one division each of 2S1 Gvozdikas, D-30s, BM-21s, and MT-12s), and the usual support components.[13]

Army Aviation

As of early 2022, the ground forces of the ZSU included an aviation component comprising four Independent Army Aviation Brigades (OBrAAs), including: 11th OBrAA in Kherson, 12th OBrAA in Novi Kalinov, 16th OBrAA in Brody, and 18th OBrAA in Poltava.

Each of the four brigades operated a mix of Mi-8MT/MTV/MSB-V and Mi-24P/PU1 helicopters, but the entire fleet included only some 30–35 of the former and 25–30 of the latter models. As clear from these designations, the ZSU attempted have these upgraded by the Ukrainian company Aviakon, in 2016–2017. The Mi-25PU1 upgrade included the installation of new engines: an indigenous, omni-directional infrared jammer and flare dispensers; the addition of a GPS receiver to the navigation system, and compatibility of the cockpit with night vision goggles. However, a further upgrade to the Mi-24PU2 standard was stopped due to the lack of funding. A total of 23 Mi-8s received similar improvements that brought them to the Mi-8MSB-V standard by 2018, and the weapons systems of both types were expanded through the addition of B-8M pods for S-8 unguided 80mm rockets, and B-13 pods for S-13 122mm rockets. About a dozen heavily modified Mi-2MSB-Vs served with the 18th OBrAA for training purposes, but could also be armed with B-8M pods.

Officially at least, the Army Aviation crews flew just 43 hours and 40 minutes per year in 2019, and 50 in 2020. Thus, most crews actually lacked continual training. However, all were combat experienced from Donbass: the Army Aviation lost five Mi-8s and Mi-24s in 2014 and 2015, while another four Mi-8s and three Mi-24 were damaged, and this attrition forced Ukrainians to stop flying helicopters over the combat zone. However, over the following years the ZSU deployed two ad-hoc units to support the United Nations' peacekeeping missions abroad. The 56th Independent Helicopter Detachment operated eight Mi-8s and six Mi-24s in Liberia between 2004 and 2018, where their crews concluded a staggering 55,000 sorties, logging 60,000 flight hours there. Furthermore, the 18th Independent Helicopter Detachment, equipped with four Mi-8MTs and four Mi-24, was involved with the UN mission in the Democratic Republic of the Congo, between 2012 and 2018, where its crews flew more than 3,000 combat sorties. Therefore, while a relatively small sub-branch, operating a rather limited quantity of lightly modified helicopters (if at all), and flying little in Ukraine, the Army Aviation was one of most battle-hardened elements of the entre ZSU.[15]

Territorial Defence

In the aftermath of the invasion of Crimea, the ZSU established several dozen battalions of Territorial Defence (TD). This experiment proved short-lived, as the mass of resulting units was staffed by volunteers and soon converted into regular motorised infantry elements of the army. Instead, in 2018, a new, much bigger Territorial Defence structure came into being, organised into battalions, and subsequently, newly established brigades. By 2020, each Oblast had its own TD brigade that controlled a varying number of minor units within its area of responsibility: in turn, every brigade was responsible to one of four Operational Commands of the army. Contrary to the National Guard (see below for details), responsibility for which lay within the realms of the Ministry of Internal Affairs, the Territorial Defence remained subjected to the Ministry of Defence and, before March 2022, its units were not supposed to operate outside their immediate area of establishment and responsibility. The entire TD was organised around a very small core of professionals and part-time servicemen and women, who underwent regular refresher courses. Virtually all citizens aged between 18 and 60 could join the force, as could foreigners staying in Ukraine for at least five years.

On 1 January 2022, the TD was converted into a distinct branch of the ZSU and saw its role further enhanced to counter the Russian 'hybrid warfare' strategy deployed successfully in 2014 and 2015. In peacetime, the Territorial Defence was to be tasked with man-made or natural disasters, while at war it was to secure rear areas, protect crucial infrastructure, combat enemy infiltrations, or organise resistance in the case of occupation. As of that time (January 2022), Kyiv planned to establish a total of 150 battalions controlled by 25 brigades, of which 24 were already existent and designated sequentially from 101 to 124. They included a cadre of about 10,000, reinforced by about 130,000 on mobilisation.

Each TD battalion was planned to be about 500 strong, divided between the headquarters section, three infantry companies, one support company, and several support platoons, armed with AKM assault rifles, PKM medium machine guns and RPGs: the heaviest weapons operated by territorial defence units were 23mm ZU-23 anti-aircraft guns.

The new structure was still a 'work in progress' when Russia invaded on 24 February 2022: much of the cadre had received no training at all, and many brigades existed on paper only. However, the very existence of the TD enabled a quick mobilisation and arming of dozens of thousands of volunteers, many of them veterans from the Donbass with extensive combat experience. By the end of March 2022, most brigades included between four and six – some as many as eight – battalions. As the subsequent developments were to show, by that point in time, personnel ceased to be a problem: instead, the mass of units lacked modern armament, equipment and gear, but especially training and competent commanders.[16]

Fully mobilised, by May 2022, the TD reached a strength of more than 300,000. As such, it significantly bolstered the regular units and reserve units of the army, which meanwhile counted between 250,000 and 300,000 personnel, equipped with at least 1,000 MBTs, 2,000 artillery pieces of 100mm calibre or higher, and several thousands of other armoured vehicles. Arguably, most heavy weapons were at least a generation behind those operated by the VSRF. In turn, the best units of the ZSU benefitted from better training, a far more advanced communication infrastructure, and such sophisticated combat gear as night vision equipment. Above all, the Ukrainians made extensive use of small UAVs for reconnaissance and artillery spotting, had a huge number of sniper teams, and officers of regular units were indoctrinated in far more flexible tactics than their Russian counterparts, authorising them to operate with higher autonomy than ever before. Their primary problem was the huge frontline they had to defend: as of early March 2022, this was nearly 2,000 kilometres long. Thanks to extensive anti-tank capabilities and the mobility of its infantry – greatly enhanced through Western supplies of advanced, man portable systems – the Ukrainian Army and Territorial Defence evolved into a unique structure, tailor-made to face a massive onslaught and conventional war in Donbass.

National Guard

Originally established in 1991, the National Guard of Ukraine (NG) was disbanded in 1999. The annexation of Crimea and beginning of the war in Donbass then pointed out the requirement for a hybrid, paramilitary force, capable of fulfilling both law enforcement and combat tasks. This resulted in the reactivation of the National Guard as a body that integrated a large number of volunteer units created in the conflict zone of 2014–2015. Right since its re-establishment, the National Guard greatly benefitted from support of Western advisors and in a matter of a few years evolved into a powerful force of around 60,000 personnel, mostly organised into specialised units (like anti-terror, and units dedicated to the protection of critical infrastructure, foremost nuclear powerplants). Administratively, all were subordinated directly to the HQ in Kyiv, but for operational purposes they were always assigned to the Operational Commands of the ZSU. As of early 2022, only about 14,000 were assigned to combat formations equipped with heavy armament and served in 'combat related' duties: they were organised into four brigades (designated 1 to 4), each of which comprised two or three infantry battalions: some were reinforced by a battalion of tanks, artillery, anti-aircraft artillery, or missiles. Furthermore, the NG included two reinforced regiments that were brigades by all but their designation. For example, the 18th 'Azov' Special Purpose Regiment included two infantry battalions, a tank battalion, and numerous training and support units operating T-64, T-72, and T-80 MBTs, BTR-4 IFVs, several types of locally manufactured MRAPs, 2S1 Gvozdika self-propelled artillery pieces, towed D-30 howitzers and ZU-23 anti-aircraft guns. That said, the average NG battalion was slightly smaller than that of the Army, and usually numbered just 300 troops. Appendix I presents known major Units of the Ukrainian Army, Territorial Defence & National Guard as of February 2022.

In addition to ground units, the National Guard included a small air arm, centred on a squadron based in Alexandria, that – as of mid-2020 – operated five Mil Mi-8MT, three Mi-8MSB-V, two Mi-2MSB and two Airbus H.225 helicopters. As the deliveries of 12 H.225s were completed, in early 2022, the second squadron came into being, operating this type only. Finally, the NG operated several transport aircraft.[17]

Ukrainian Air Power

Officially established on 17 March 1992, the Ukrainian Air Force (*Povitryani Syly Ukrayiny*; PSU) inherited no fewer than 2,800 aircraft organised into 49 regiments and 11 independent squadrons from the former Soviet Air Force. This inventory was massively reduced during the 1990s: by the early 2000s, the PSU was reorganised into brigades, and launched several overhaul and modernisation projects. Nevertheless, its readiness and combat effectiveness had reached rock bottom by 2014. For example, the entire 7th Tactical Aviation Brigade had only 10 operational Sukhoi Su-24Ms and Su-24MRs as of February that year. Despite its poor condition, the Air Force operated intensively during the war in Donbass and suffered heavy losses to Russian air defences, including one Antonov An-26 transport, two MiG-29 fighter-bombers (ASCC/NATO-codename 'Fulcrum'), one Su-24M light bomber (ASCC/NATO-codename 'Fencer'), and five Sukhoi Su-25 attack aircraft (ASCC/NATO-codename 'Frogfoot').

With the acquisition of entirely new aircraft remaining unaffordable, by 2015 this triggered a rush to recover as many airframes to operational condition as possible with the help of the local aeronautical industry. As a result, while the PSU received only two overhauled aircraft and helicopters in 2013, and eight in 2014, 20 followed in 2015, 14 in 2016, and 22 in 2017. By early 2019, the Air Force operated a total of 155 fighter-bombers.

A much bigger issue proved to be an upgrade of the PSU's ageing MiGs and Sukhois. In 2007, Kyiv contracted the Lviv State Aviation Maintenance Plant (LDARZ) with an upgrade of MiG-29s. This resulted in the version designated MiG-29MU1, the first prototype of which flew in 2011. The new standard included a major upgrade of the fire-control system, new navigation and new communication systems, but lacked the planned improvement of the N019 radar to make it compatible with the R-27ET1 air-to-air missiles developed by the Aryom Corporation, which had a claimed range of 95km. The situation was slightly better in the case of Ukrainian Sukhoi Su-27 interceptors (ASCC/NATO-codename 'Flanker'). Carried out by the MiGremont company from 2012, this resulted in the version designated the Su-27M1, which added a GPS and GLONASS receiver to the navigation system, a new radio, an improved helmet-mounted display, an increase in the detection range of the N001 radar by 30 percent, and the addition of digital cockpit displays. However, eight years later only 11 aircraft had been modified to that standard. Starting in 2008, 12 of the Ukrainian fleet of Su-25 armoured attack aircraft were brought up to the Su-25M1K standard, which included a new navigation suite, new (digital) fire-control system and head-up-display – while the entire fleet was equipped with newly designed Adros KUV 26-50-0 flare dispensers.

The lack of funding had its impact not only on the process of upgrading the PSU's combat aircraft fleet but on training of its flying and ground personnel. Flight hours were allocated parsimoniously, each crew undertaking about 50 hours a year at most for much of the previous 20 years. To reach at least such results, the PSU carried out an upgrade of its Aero L-39C Albatross training jets, resulting in the L-39M1 variant. In addition to being powered by AI-25TLSh engines, this included a new avionics suite, virtually converting the type into a flying simulator for MiG-29s and Su-27s. Correspondingly, several L-39M1s were assigned to each of the brigades, enabling their pilots to log precious flight hours at a much lower price than if flying their actual mounts. However, even then, the mass of the L-39C fleet – operated by the 203rd Training Brigade – only received their regular periodic overhauls: as of early 2019, this was down to 16 operational L-39Cs and one L-39M1 (out of a total of 46 aircraft of this type still in service).

That said – as far as it was affordable and whenever undertaken – tactical training of Ukrainian combat pilots experienced a dramatic change. Contrary to earlier times, they flew at low altitudes, with minimal- or no support from the ground control, and frequently trained operating their aircraft from alternative airfields and highways, as recalled by one of them: 'It was an interesting experience and a pretty difficult task; we also used different airfields, non-familiar airfields, and flew some difficult routes. It was very useful for us.'[18]

Table 4: PSU, Average Flight Time per Crew

Year	Air Force	Army Aviation	Naval Aviation
2015	53hrs 49min	98hrs 13min	52hrs 07min
2016	42hrs 23min	54hrs 52min	34hrs 58min
2017	50hrs 01min	51hrs 49min	40hrs 31min
2019	32hrs 35min	43hrs 40min	34hrs 01min
2020	43hrs 40min	50hrs 00min	22hrs 59min

At least some influx of additional experience and new tactical methods came through the PSU's participation in multinational exercises, especially Clear Sky 2018, during which Boeing F-15C Eagle interceptors of the California Air National Guard's 144th Fighter Wing were involved. By simulating Russian-operated Sukhoi Su-30 and Su-35s, they helped the Ukrainians adapt to the new threat and develop suitable tactics to counter them. According to major General Clay Garrison, former Commander of the California Air National Guard and director of that exercise, Ukrainian pilots impressed their US partners, despite their limited flight time:

> … really it was about everything we do in Western-style tactical aviation, and expose the Ukrainians to all of that. We did plenty of basic fighter manoeuvres with our F-15Cs against their MiG-29s and Su-27s and to be honest we could tell instantly that their pilots were very good. They are very tactically inventive, they know their airframes and also understand what they are lacking. I mean, they fly old jets. […] When I flew with them I thought their airmanship and the way they moved their aircraft – especially close-in dogfighting – was incredible. They knew their aircraft as well as anyone else knows their aircraft. I have fought Fulcrums and Flankers from other countries and they were up there with the best of the people that fly those airframes – hands down. But what we did in terms of Clear Sky was us trying to introduce them to mixing all the assets together.[19]

As of 2019, the PSU was organised into six brigades and one independent squadron, that operated a total of 60 MiG-29 and 35 Su-27s, 32 Su-25s and 28 Su-24M/MRs, 23 An-26s and three An-30s, eight Ilyushin Il-76MDs, and one Tupolev Tu-135 VIP-transporter, as well as at least 15 Mi-2 and Mi-8 helicopters. By early 2022, the organisation of the force remained the same, but the number of operational combat aircraft decreased to 37 MiG-29s, 23 Su-24Ms and Su-24MRs, 31 Su-25s and 34 Su-27s.

Growing UAV Fleet

As of 2014, the ZSU had very few unmanned aerial vehicles, and PSU had next to none in operational service. While the army was quick to acquire up to 64 unmanned aircraft of different types by 2019, and another 46 by 2020, the Air Force was lagging behind. During the Donbass War its primary reconnaissance assets were old Antonov An-30s and Sukhoi Su-24MRs: the former were equipped for mapping, but the latter could carry BKR-1 photoreconnaissance and Fantasmagoria-B ELINT-gathering pods. The Air Force's first dedicated UAV unit – the 383rd Independent UAV Regiment – was established in 2016 and initially operated a small number of antiquated Tupolev Tu-141 and Tu-143 UAVs, overhauled and returned to service during the Russian aggression.[20] A major breakthrough in this regards took place only in 2019, when the PSU acquired its first batch of six Bayraktar TB.2s from Turkey, and then placed an additional order. By February 2022, a total of 36 Turkish-made UAVs were in operational service – both by the Air Force and the Navy.

Integrated Air Defence System

Considering the sheer size of Ukraine's airspace, the inherent weaknesses of its Air Force, and the fact that its armed forces traced their origins to those of the former Soviet army, it is unsurprising that ground-based systems bore the brunt of the air defence. Indeed, it was in this regards that the ZSU underwent the perhaps most important transformation between 2014 and 2022 – even if this remained largely unrecognised in public.

As in the former USSR, the task of air defence was originally distributed between two branches: the ground forces were responsible for air defence over the frontlines, while the air defence force protected the airspace deeper over the country. In 2004, the air defence force was merged with the Air Force. Lighter and mobile systems – like MANPADS, Strela-10, and Osa-AKMs, were all assigned to the army, and served to protect of its mobile units, while heavier systems – like the S-125 Pechora, Buk M1 and S-300 – were assigned to the PSU. The mass was manufactured back in the 1980s but subjected to overhauls and modifications by local industry. Between 2015 and 2020, a total of 138 surface-to-air missile systems were delivered to the PSU, enabling it to expand through the establishment of additional units: correspondingly, by 2017 it operated four air defence brigades and five air defence regiments, where each of the latter operated several 'divisions' (i.e. batteries).

Operationally, the PSU was organised into four Air Commands (ACs), each with its own airspace control and reporting centre (ACRC):

- West, HQ in Lviv (193rd ACRC)
- East, HQ in Dnipro (196th ACRC)
- South, HQ in Odessa (195th ACRC)
- Centre, HQ in Vasylkiv (192nd ACRC)

Since 2016, each AC had its own radio-technical brigade, equipped with early warning radars (1st, 14th, 138th, and 164th), with the help of which it exercised control over manned interceptors and ground-based air defence units, as listed in Table 5. In this fashion, by 2022, the PSU established an integrated air defence system (IADS) consisting of four sub-systems, within which MiG-29 and Su-27 manned interceptors represented the first line of defence; S-300 SAMs were responsible for long-range engagements, and Buk M1s and S-125 Pechoras for medium- and short-range engagements. A combination of these assets became capable of not only defending the airspace from enemy aircraft, but also from attacks by low-flying cruise missiles. However, there remained the problem related to the overall size of the Ukrainian airspace and the number of urban

Table 5: Ukrainian Air Force, Army Aviation, Naval Aviation and National Guard

Unit	Base	Notes
Air Force		
7th Brigade	Starokonstantyniv	directly subordinated; 1st and 2nd Squadrons with 19 Su-24M, 3rd Squadron with 9 Su-24MR
15th Brigade	Boryspil IAP	directly subordinated; 1 Tu-134, 3 An-30, 5 An-26, 4 Mi-8
25th Brigade	Melitopol	directly subordinated; 1 An-26, 8 Il-76MD
39th Squadron	Ozernoye	3 Su-27P/M1/UB, L-39M1; status in early 2022 unclear
203rd Brigade	Chuguyev	16 L-39C, 1 L-39M1, 8 An-26, 2 Mi-2, 2 Mi-8
456th Brigade	Vinnitsya	9 An-26, 7 Mi-8
AC West		
114th Brigade	Ivano-Frankivsk AB	18 MiG-29, 3 MiG-29UB, 1–2 L-39M1
11th Air Defence Regiment	Shepetivka	Buk M1
223rd Air Defence Regiment	Strvi	Buk M1
540th Air Defence Regiment	Kamianka Buzka	S-300PS
AC East		
138th Air Defence Brigade	Dnipro	S-300PS
301st Air Defence Regiment	Nikopol	S-300PS
AC South		
204th Brigade	Kulbakyne	12 MiG-29, 3 MiG-29UB, 1–2 L-39M1
299th Brigade	Kulbakyne	16 Su-25, 3 Su-25M1, 6 Su-25M1K, 7 Su-25UB/UBM1/UBM1K
160th Air Defence Brigade	Odessa	S-300PM
208th Air Defence Brigade	Kherson	S-300PS, Buk M1
201st Air Defence Regiment	Pervomaisk	S-300PS
AC Centre		
40th Brigade	Vasylkiv	9 MiG-29, 11 MiG-29MU1, 4 MiG-29UB, 1–2 L-39M1
831st Brigade	Myrohorod	22 Su-27P/M1/UB (2 squadrons), 1–2 L-39M1
96th Air Defence Brigade	Danylivka	S-300PS
156th Air Defence Regiment	Zolotonosha	Buk M1
National Guard Aviation		
? Squadron		15 Mi-8MT/MSB-V, Mi-2MSB-V
? Squadron		12 H.225

centres and strategic installations that had to be protected: the PSU neither had enough manned interceptors nor SAMs to properly protect anything more than the Kyiv, Kharkiv and Odessa areas. Other major urban centres – but especially numerous oil refineries, depots for petrol, oil and lubricants, many major military bases and especially major ammunition dumps – all lacked protection other than a battery or two of anti-aircraft guns, perhaps a team or two operating MANPADs. Moreover, as subsequent experience was to show, the Russian Air-Space Force was well-equipped to overcome even the densest of Ukrainian air defence: the latter were unable to combat all kinds of threat, even less so at once.

Mosquito Fleet

The Ukrainian Navy was in a state of decay at the time Russia seized Crimea: Kyiv was unable to fund the sustainment of assets inherited from the former USSR, and then the loss of major bases and assets in Sevastopol further crippled the force, leaving it without crucial infrastructure and ships. Remaining assets were redeployed to Odessa and Mariupol, but these were almost exclusively light units. On 25 November 2018, the Ukrainian Navy was involved in an incident with its Russian counterpart, in which the latter prevented two Gurza-M-class gunboats and a trailer from transiting the Kerch Strait, and then opened fire, wounding six sailors. All three ships were captured, but later released. Moscow did relinquish a few of the warships captured in 2014, but the Ukrainian Navy remained a tiny affair. As of 2021, its largest warships were:

- Project-1135.1-class frigate *Hetman Sagajdachny*
- Project 1124P-class frigate *Vinnitsyia*
- Project 1258-class minesweeper *Genichesk*
- Landing ship of the Project 773-class
- Project 304-class support ship *Donbass*

All these vessels were designed and constructed during the times of the Soviet Union and – because the establishment of a 'blue water navy' remained unaffordable – they were never upgraded: the sole frigate was undergoing repairs in Mykolaiv as of February 2022. Instead, during the eight years of the Donbass War, Ukrainian Navy focused on developing a so-called 'mosquito fleet': one made up of small patrol vessels, fast missile craft, and a few amphibious boats, capable of providing at least a minimal denial capability against the powerful Black Sea Fleet of the Russian Federation. That said, even this mosquito fleet did not grow fast enough. As of early 2022, only a single Project 206MP-class fast missile craft (FAC), *Priluki*, four Island-class patrol craft acquired from the USA in 2019–2021, and seven Project 58155 Gurza-M-class gunboats constructed since 2016 were in service (the latter were relatively powerful vessels, mounting an automatic gun, a heavy machine gun, a grenade launcher, and two laser-guided anti-tank missiles). An additional 13 Gurza-M-class boats and two British-made Sandown minehunters were on order, and their deliveries planned for 2022: these were to be followed by several Ada-class corvettes ordered in Turkey in 2020. The only other important development of the last few years before the Russian aggression was the development of the shore-based Neptune anti-ship missiles, conducted by the Luch Corporation since 2013. The first test-firings took place in 2018, and the first prototype battery – including just one launcher for four missiles, a command truck, and two resupply vehicles – was delivered to the Navy in 2020, with three other batteries planned to follow in 2022.[21]

In addition to surface vessels, the Ukrainian Navy operated a small aviation arm, centred on the 10th Naval Aviation Brigade. Established in 2004 and – since 2014 – based at Kulbakino AB, outside Mykolaiv, this was equipped with at least four Mi-8MSB-Vs, and between five and eight Mil Mi-14s, Kamov Ka-27s, and Ka-226s. A pair of ancient Antonov An-2 biplane transports and several Beriev Be-12 amphibians were still maintained, but had not flown in years. Nevertheless, following its order for six Bayraktar TB.2s, in 2019, the Navy expected to become a major use of UAVs and UCAVs.[22]

2
PUTIN *AKTIENGESELLSCHAFT*[1]

The birth and death of states is something that rarely occurs, and when one or the other happens, it does so in different political contexts, resulting in contradictory practices. Nominally at least, the United Nations have regulated such occurrences through the customary law and two conventions on state succession, thus making sure the replacement of one state by another is regulated in regards of responsibility for international relations of the territory in question.[2] In the case of the dissolution of the USSR, it was the Russian Federation that declared itself to be, 'the continuator state of the USSR', on the grounds that it contained 51 percent of the population and 77 percent of the territory. This claim was accepted by most of the former states of the USSR, resulting in President Yeltsin's announcement of 24 December 1991 that the Soviet membership in the Security Council of the UN, and all other United Nations organs, would be continued by the Russian Federation, and that all the Soviet embassies would become Russian embassies.[3]

Early years of the Armed Forces of the Russian Federation
It was for such and similar reasons that the Russian Federation inherited the biggest share of the once mighty Soviet armed forces – which promptly proved a two-edged sword, because a series of shocks then plunged the Russian economy into one crisis after another, landing vast segments of the population in poverty. While most industry ended up in the possession of the so-called 'oligarchs', the administration of President Yeltsin grew both authoritarian and corrupt. Unsurprisingly, for much of the 1990s, the Armed Forces of the Russian Federation (*Vooruzhonnije Sily Rossiyskoj Federatsii*, VSRF) – officially established in March 1992 – went through similar experiences. On one hand, the VSRF had to repatriate the mass of its best units and troops from Eastern Europe and find new bases on Russian territory; on the other, the withdrawal from Eastern Europe, the Baltic republics and former Soviet states of Belarus and Ukraine meant the loss of a huge number of major military facilities. Finally, with an end of the confrontation with NATO, Moscow no longer had any purpose in maintaining a force of over two million men and women under arms.

However, the required downsizing caused severe unrest within the officer corps, resulting in this process being neither cohesive nor well-planed: instead, it consisted of a series of reforms tied to the changing priorities of the Yeltsin administration. To prevent dissent, perhaps even a military coup, Moscow curbed the mass of its ambitions of changing the organisation and doctrine. The VSRF thus remained – essentially – the 'Soviet armed forces light': a force organised into eight military districts but centred on 85 divisions of the army, the most important of which were airborne troops and artillery, and in which a full third out of 670,000 troops were officers. Endemic lack of funding had devastating effects upon the state of equipment, readiness and morale: the majority of officers and NCOs were frequently not paid for months; entire garrisons were unable to pay their bills for electricity or buy food to feed their troops and were rendered incapable of undergoing even the most basic training. Gradually, corruption spread to a point where by the early 2000s it was eating as much as 40 percent of the defence budget; where the abuse of recruits went through the roof, and the draft dodging became widespread.

The Russian Point of View
Amid the growing chaos and deep shame, the VSRF became entangled in a number of wars fuelled by what can be described as the 'Russian point of view'. According to this point of view, Russia is the greatest nation of all and there is no need to envy anybody or anything; Russians can achieve anything – if they only find it worth trying – and, the Russians are internationalists while everybody else is nationalist. Primarily, Russia is always right.

Unsurprisingly, in 1992, Russian nationalists sparked a civil war in Molodova, and brought the part of the country east of the Dniester River under their control, unilaterally declaring the 'Pridnestorvian Moldova Republic' – or Transnistria – as an independent country. Around the same time, the 201st Motor Rifle Division helped establish a post-Soviet dictatorship in power in Tajikistan. While these adventures were successful, the next one was not: in 1994, the VSRF was deployed to topple the authorities of Chechnya – a part of the Russian Federation – only to encounter fierce resistance and suffer severe casualties. Grozny, the capitol of the federal republic, was overrun after three weeks of bitter fighting, in which up to 35,000 civilians were killed, but the insurgency remained intact and spread into neighbouring parts of Russia. Indeed, in 1996, the Chechens managed to infiltrate Grozny and take it back, forcing the Russians to besiege the city and ruin it completely by air strikes and artillery barrages. Only this action paved the way to a peace deal granting wide autonomy to the republic, in exchange for it remaining a part of the federation.

By late 1999, the new strongman in the Kremlin, Vladimir Putin, concluded this to be insufficient. After provoking a new war, he launched a three-pronged invasion supported by immense volumes of firepower. At the cost of massive civilian casualties, the Russians drove the insurgents into the mountains of southern Chechnya, until a combination of Russian-style counterinsurgency operations – mainly a brutal repression resulting in the emigration of about 50 percent of the population, and bribery of those who were still around – subdued the uprising. Nominally at least, this Second Chechen War ended with the imposition of pro-Russian leader Ramazan Kadyrov – in a ruined Grozny – in 2005.[4]

Serdyukov's Problems with the GenStab

Having won a war, and then the elections that confirmed his position as the President of the Russian Federation, in 2006 Putin felt strong enough to embark on – amongst other things – a reform of the VSRF. When his first Minister of Defence, Sergei Ivanov (a former KGB official and Putin's close associate), failed to effect the expected change, in 2007 he was replaced by Anatoly Eduardovich Serdyukov. However, while attempting to bring defence spending under control, curb corruption and inefficiency, Serdyukov promptly collided with the powerful General Staff of the Armed Forces of the Russian Federation (GenStab): the latter not only opposed the appointment of a civilian with no military background, but fiercely countered his attempts to combat corruption.

Barely a year after assuming his new position – and although leaving the daily administration of troops and strategic and operational planning to military officers – Serdyukov found himself in charge of the VSRF when Putin ordered an invasion of Georgia. The short war was quickly won by Russia, driving many to the wrong conclusion about this being a confirmation of improved conditions and effectiveness of the 'reorganised' armed forces. Certainly enough, the Russian forces won a resounding victory without significant numerical superiority, while securing separatist-controlled South Ossetia and Abkhazia, and thus preventing Georgia from joining NATO.[5] However, this operation revealed a number of shortcomings – like lack of reconnaissance, lack of advanced navigation systems, a complete breakdown in communication systems, poor training of professional Russian troops in comparison to professional Georgian troops, or the fact that up to 70 percent of the deployed MBTs broke down – that even the contemporary Chief of the General Staff, Army General Nikolay Makarov, openly acknowledged that the VSRF was unable to fight a modern war.[6]

New Look

As a result of such conclusions – and by auditing members of the GenStab for their physical fitness – Serdyukov gradually overcame some of the resistance and pushed through a few of his reforms, widely known as the *novy oblik* (new look/appearance). These primarily focused on a transformation of the VSRF from a mass-mobilisation army to a small force of combat-ready contract soldiers. Correspondingly, the entire structure was streamlined over the next four years: the number of military regions was reduced to four joint strategic Operational Commands (OSKs) capable of coordinating the operations of units from all branches deployed within their territory of operations. While the special forces (*Spetsnaz*), Airborne Assault Troops (VDV), and the Strategic Forces remained directly subordinated to the Ministry of Defence, the army structure was drastically simplified. At the intermediate level between OSKs and manoeuvre formations, Serdyukov retained so-called Combined Arms Armies (CAAs). In turn, he disbanded all the cadre units and all the 24 divisions (except for one specialised in the defence of the Kurile Islands) and replaced them with 85 brigades and two bases (the latter two were deployed in Armenia and Tajikistan). In grand total, the VSRF had the number of its major units reduced from 1,890 to just 172, and its manpower reduced to about one million. While the service of conscripts was shortened from 18 to 12 months and they were no longer recalled for refresher training after their national service, Serdyukov intended to man most brigades with so-called *kontraktniki* – contract, or professional soldiers – which were expected to staff between 70 and 90 percent of the authorised strength of all the brigades.

Serdyukov's reforms enabled the VSRF to fight limited conflicts, and to retain the ability to engage in a large-scale war with a peer opponent, though remaining reliant on conscription to bolster the core of professionals and trained reservists. That said, the Russian armed forces thus found themselves in a situation comparable to that of the French army during the Cold War: they fielded a relatively large conventional force manned by conscripts, while organised into limited-size professional contingents available for short-term, expeditionary operations only. The French reacted by splitting their army into two; on the contrary, in 2012, Putin replaced Serdyukov with one of his favourites, Sergei Shoygu, and the two then went a step further: they took measures to make military careers more attractive and managed to raise the number of the *kontraktniki* in their ground forces from 186,000 in 2012 to 300,000 in 2013, and then to 405,100 in 2020. With the number of officers kept at around 220,000 through the same period, this gave them about 770,000 troops available for ground combat in total. Out of about 230,000 in the ground forces, no fewer than 130,000 were professionals – including the *kontraktniki* and officers. Furthermore, since the Russian military intervention in Syria in the summer of 2015, they tasked several of Putin's confidantes with the establishment of private military contractor (PMC) companies – even though these were, at least officially, strictly forbidden by law (for details see below).[7]

Reversal of Reforms: the Shoygu Era

Serdyukov's fast-paced reforms, attempts to curb corruption, and resulting disagreements with large parts of the VSRF officer corps were not the only reason for his removal: at least as important was the fact that he proved willing to purchase arms and equipment abroad whenever the domestic defence sector failed to provide these at necessary quality and an affordable price. For example, in 2011, he placed an order for two Mistral-class amphibious assault ships in France; in other cases, he refused to order obsolete or unnecessary weapons systems merely in order to secure the political loyalty of corporations or their workforce. As such, he became unwanted in Putin's system of shareholding oligarchs, whose priority was extracting their own cut from state-sponsored contracts. On the contrary, Shoygu proved eager to please the officer corps by promoting or reinstating those removed by Serdyukov, by re-establishing historic units – including numerous divisions – and by pleasing the higher strata of the defence sector.

The later fact was quite ironic, considering it was nobody other than Putin who – starting back in the mid-2000s – began imposing himself in control of the mass of the Russian defence sector through establishing (usually by decree) state-controlled conglomerates for almost every branch of the arms industry. The boards of these conglomerates were usually staffed by his favourites – often by poets and philosophers, and next to never by anybody with suitable education, experience, or skills in industrial management – the task of which was to exercise control in Putin's name and secure his (and their) cut of the profit. The latter issue was of particular importance because unlike the 1990s, when next to no new equipment was purchased, starting in 2008, Putin, buoyed by the increase in oil and gas prices, placed massive orders for arms. Over the following years, the Russian defence budget was continuously increased, from about 12.5 percent gross national product in 2012, to 14.5 percent in 2014. The trend of channelling ever more of the state's income into the acquisition of new equipment was continued through the following

BATTALION TACTICAL GROUPS

The GenStab's solution to the 'two tier' recruitment system introduced by Serdyukov was the reorganisation of available brigades and divisions: instead of their usual elements, each of these were to establish several task forces – or *batalonnaja takticheskaja gruppa* (Battalion Tactical Group, BTG) – manned exclusively by professionals: BTGs were kept at a high state of readiness and could be deployed for operations at quick notice, and in situations where the involvement of conscript troops was deemed politically inopportune for Putin. As a result, although very few brigades ever reached 100 percent of their manpower even as of 2020, each had at least two – often three or more – BTGs ready for deployment. The number of such task forces grew from 66 in 2016, to 168 in 2021, and then to more than 170 in 2022.

That said, the BTGs were much more than mere tools for the concentration of professionals: instead, they were the continuation of decades-old practices dating back to the times of the Second World War and, indeed were similar to the essence of the *Wehrmacht*'s ad-hoc *Kampfgruppe*. Such task forces were routinely formed not only by the Soviet army, but by the Cuban, French, South African and US armed forces, amongst others. That said, the BTGs established by the VSRF since the mid-2010s were task-oriented and relatively flexible, combined arms formations, packing as much firepower, reconnaissance, and logistical assets as necessary to enable short-duration expeditionary operations for independent formations. For example, a typical BTG from a Motor Rifle Brigade was based on the organisation of a single motor rifle battalion, reinforced by two or three artillery batteries and a company each of tanks, engineers, anti-aircraft defence, and reconnaissance, plus various support platoons. As a result, the nominal strength of each BTG varied widely, from about 650 to 900 troops – although their average strength was often between 400 and 500 due to chronical shortages of the *kontraktniki*. The formation of permanent battalion tactical groups had its negative sides, too, mainly in their command structures, the logistics system and thus their staying power. To alleviate such factors, for major operations the VSRF established about a dozen specialised command brigades, capable of controlling the operations of several BTGs. That said, the most critical flaw in this concept was that it 'sucked' the best equipment and personnel from parent units, while rendering their remnants as undeployable pools.[9]

Unsurprisingly, the first few BTGs deployed in action during the Russo-Georgian War of 2008, and especially those that saw actions in the Donbass during 2014–2015, experienced significant problems whenever involved in protracted operations. One result of this experience was the decision to re-establish divisions in 2016. Even if lighter than their ancestors – and including about 7,000 troops, instead of the earlier 10,000–13,000 troops – the divisions had large headquarters and logistics elements, and thus proved better able to support the BTGs in operations.

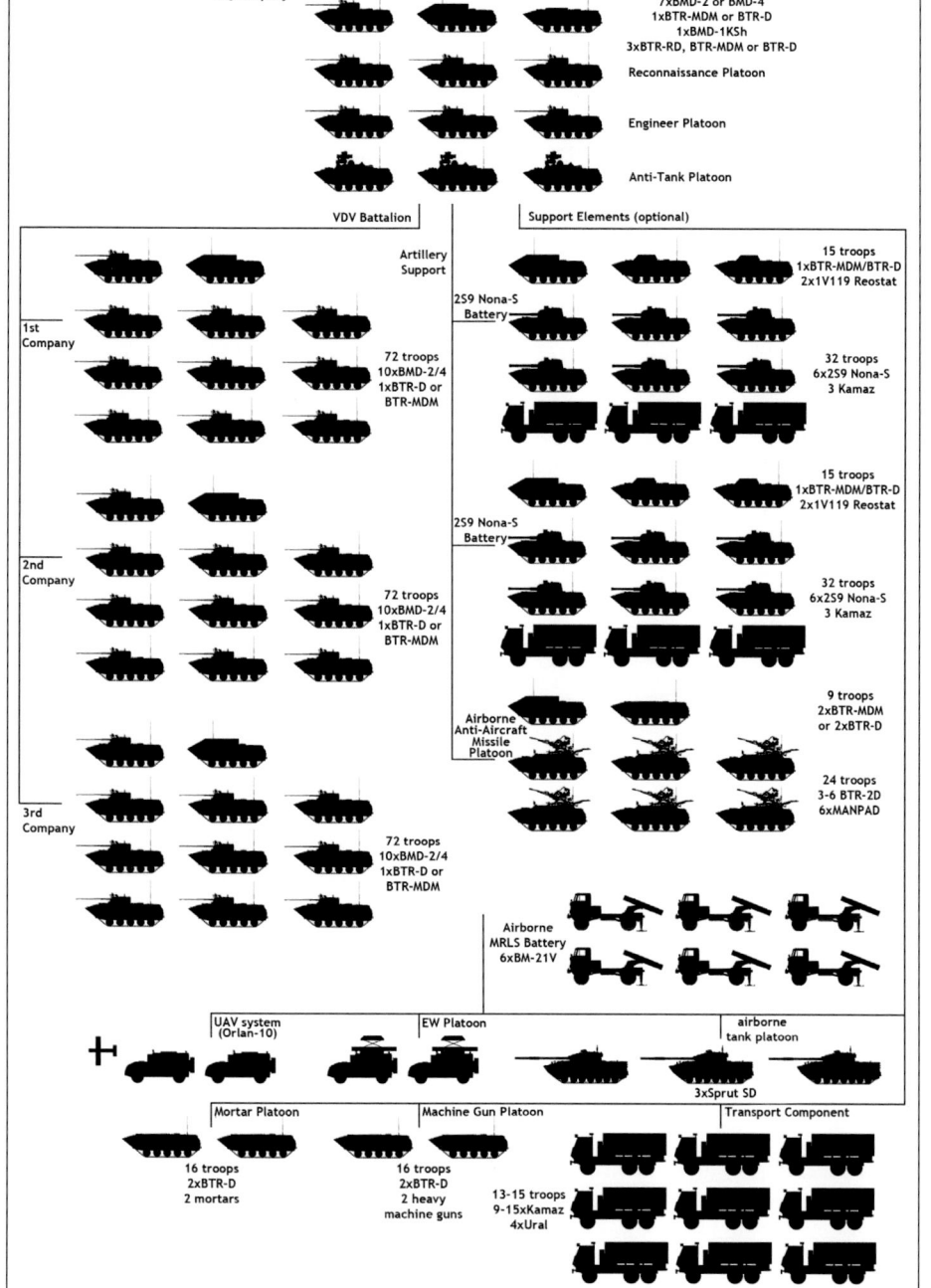

A diagram showing the nominal – indeed: 'best case' – composition of a BTG of Airborne Assault Troops of the VSRF. In reality, and due to the critical shortage of troops, the mass of BTGs deployed to Ukraine starting in February 2022, went into action with about half this complement. (Diagram by Tom Cooper)

eight years, underlining the fact that possession of powerful and well-equipped armed forces was high on Putin's priority list: or, in other words, that his aspirations to impose the Russian Federation as a global player and powerbroker were very much obvious even at the time the strongman in Moscow maintained friendly – in some cases cordial – relations with the majority of Western governments.

Because the simultaneous downsizing of the ground forces resulted in block retirement of older weapons systems, the VSRF found itself flushed with new equipment. Troops were issued with the new generation *Ratnik* gear, and equipped with nearly 2,000 newly constructed MBTs, a similar number of at least modified infantry fighting vehicles and armoured personnel carriers, plentiful modern artillery and multiple rocket launchers, electronic warfare and advanced air defence systems; the share of modern equipment within the VSRF increased from about 16 percent in 2010, to 61 percent in 2018, and then 70 percent in 2020.

However, the 'pristine' condition of the equipment of the Russian armed forces was deceptive. In fact, the entire program of rebuilding was fraught with difficulties. First, although Putin did invest billions into modernisation of the armed forces, the fact was that Russia's gross domestic product was comparable with that of Australia, Canada, or, after 2014, Spain. Thus, the Kremlin could never afford a true and complete modernisation of all the branches of the VSRF. This was even less possible because – in order to keep everybody satisfied and loyal – Putin assigned the same share of the defence budget to all major branches of the armed forces, and at the same time pushed for modernisation of Strategic Forces, Ground Forces, the Air Force and the Navy. However, it was a fact was that, for example, the aircraft demanded by the Air Force were significantly more expensive than tanks and artillery demanded by the army; and the training of their crews was far more expensive than training of tank crews and gunners. This disbalance was bound to trigger more or less deliberate trade-offs, such as the siphoning of available funds into inducting new equipment at the expense of operational preparedness, training, or the constitution of stocks of all kinds. Ironically, contemporary Russia emulated in this regard practices that had been endemic in the Soviet Union.

The second major problem came from within the heavily politicised defence sector, where efficiency was largely ignored. The traditional lack of reliability in delivering precisely what the customer ordered and paid for became almost legendary as boards of incompetent directors proved a major hindrance in running high-technology enterprises of the early twenty-first century: not only was their decision making ill-advised and slow, but combined with Putin's practice of extracting his cut at every opportunity, they made investment into research and development nearly impossible. Combined with the traditional weak spot of Russian industry in regards of advanced technologies, this resulted in even the most sensitive high-end products – like Sukhoi Su-30 and Su-35 interceptors, not to mention MBTs and guided missiles – becoming completely dependent on the installation of electronics imported from Ukraine or the West. Unsurprisingly, the Russians experienced massive problems while trying to research and develop a new generation of weapons systems, whether intercontinental ballistic missiles, fighter-bombers, or military-grade UAVs, and eventually ended up purchasing related technology and know-how from abroad. The situation only worsened in 2014, when, due to Putin's invasion of Ukraine, the Russian defence sector was suddenly cut off from about 150 major Ukrainian enterprises researching and developing new weapons systems for it, and this was then followed by a Western embargo on exports of high technologies. Already

bled white of skilled workforce and talent back in the 1990s, the Russian defence sector proved unable to even reverse-engineer urgently necessary electronics, never mind developing substitutes or new weapons systems: instead, it became overdependent on using technology literally smuggled from abroad. Combined with chronic underfunding and lack of industrial management skills, the end result was the failure to field the planned new generation of weaponry, such as the T-14 Armata main battle tank/universal combat platform, the Boomerang APC, or the Sukhoi Su-57 'stealth' fighter. In this regards, even a massive propaganda campaign could not hide the fact that they were all extremely expensive, and that the research and development of their major components lagged years behind schedule. Unsurprisingly, for all of the 2010s, the Russian defence sector thus proved capable only of rolling out ever further upgrades of designs dating back to the 1970s and 1980s – such as the Su-30, Su-34, and Su-35 interceptors and fighter-bombers, T-72 MBTs, BMP-3 and BTR-82 APCs – with which it was familiar. For all practical purposes, the 'massive modernisation' of the VSRF actually meant that the force continued lagging behind the West.[8] To maintain a different impression though, during the late 2010s, the Kremlin sponsored numerous show projects that led nowhere beyond the prototype/demonstration stage, and organised ever bigger parades, leaving ever less funding for the pay and tactical training of the force.

Donbass Crucible
This 'partially reformed' VSRF was deployed during combat operations in Ukraine in 2014. Certainly enough, the Spetsnaz quickly overran the Crimea – mainly because in the political void and unpreparedness of the ZSU, there was no resistance. The sloppy response from Kyiv and shrugs from the West then encouraged Moscow to up the ante by first supporting disparate groups of separatists in the Donbass, and then launching a military intervention in their favour. Major action by the Russian armed forces began during the night of 23 to 24 August, when up to eight BTGs – including one equipped with 2S4 Tyulipan 240mm mortars – reinforced the insurgents besieging Luhansk Airport. A desperate (and costly) counterattack by the Ukrainian 1st Tank Brigade enabled the garrison to make good its escape, but other VSRF forces then encircled four brigades in the Ilovaisk area. Although the Ukrainians managed to break through, they lost half their number in the process. Together with the destruction of a Ukrainian armoured battalion at Novoazovsk, this string of victories led to the Minsk I Accord of 5 September 2014, which – essentially – froze large operations for several months. In mid-January 2015, the VSRF hit the Ukrainians at Donetsk Airport, forcing the garrison to escape in small groups, and then four Russian BTGs threatened to encircle a group of Ukrainian units centred around the 128th Mountain Assault Brigade at Debaltseve, causing them heavy losses and forcing them into a retreat. Although the war went on for the following eight years, these two offensives – in the summer of 2014 and winter of 2015 – saw its most intensive fighting, and both were concluded in favour of the strongman in Kremlin.

Indeed, the significantly improved performance of the VSRF during the two campaigns stunned many observers in the West: its BTGs were deploying massive amounts of firepower, and they proved highly flexible as dozens were quickly rotated in and out of Donbass, thus providing much of the ground force with invaluable combat experience. Improved T-72B3 and T-90 MBTs clearly outmatched their older counterparts in Ukrainian service. Moreover, the new generation of Russian-made ATGMs easily defeated even those ZSU

A Su-35S streaming its braking parachute on landing after an air combat patrol over Syria in April 2016. This type became the first true multi-role fighter-bomber to enter service with the VKS. (Russian MOD)

main battle tanks equipped with explosive reactive armour (ERA). However, what impressed the most was the massive deployment of electronic warfare (EW) and UAVs. EW paralysed the Ukrainian formations, made their coordination impossible, and disabled their UAVs, while Russian UAVs guided the fire of mobile artillery and MRLSs with devastating effects. Russian EW capabilities came as an especially big surprise, because they not only disrupted Ukrainian reconnaissance efforts, but jammed even the electronic fuses of artillery shells, and proved capable of detecting and tracking the full spectrum of radio, Wi-Fi, and GSM communications. The final shock was the speed of deployment of the Russian artillery: the efficiency of the VSRF's reconnaissance-fire complex was such that Ukrainian units were hit within 3 and 15 minutes of their localisation, and that with murderous effectiveness: up to 80 percent of ZSU casualties were caused by artillery fire.[10]

A Gamble in Syria

Only months after – temporarily – concluding its intervention in Ukraine, Moscow launched a similar intervention in favour of the embattled regime of Hafez al-Assad in Syria. Exploiting an opportunity offered by Western lack of interest in the country and the Middle East in general, Putin skilfully distracted the public at home away from effects of Western sanctions and diplomatic isolation imposed in reaction to his actions in Ukraine, gambling to bolster the myth of himself as a great strategist and military leader, and about the VSRF's invincibility in the resulting power vacuum. Russia began deploying its forces in Syria through August and September 2015: covertly, it first brought in a BTG of the 810th Naval Infantry Brigade to stop the insurgent advance on Latakia. Nearby, special forces and engineers secured Hmeimim AB, to which the Russian Air-Space Force (*Vozdushno-kosmicheskiye sily*, VKS) then deployed 32 aircraft and 14 helicopters.[11] Following extensive preparations – necessary by the ad-hoc nature of the entire enterprise – the latter went into action in late September of the same year in the form of an aerial onslaught against civic authorities, food depots, medical facilities, and water purification installations in insurgent-controlled areas, aiming to make life miserable for millions of Syrians that refused to live under Assadist oppression. After massacring thousands and driving dozens of thousands into fleeing over the border to Turkey, the VKS began bombing the positions of Syrian insurgents – with mediocre effectiveness. The Main Directorate of the General Staff of the Armed Forces of the Russian Federation (formerly the Main Intelligence Directorate, and still commonly known by its previous abbreviation, GRU) actually had no clue about who-was-who in Syria, and the available means of intelligence gathering were poor to the level where it had to rely upon information provided by Assadist services, dominated by the Islamic Revolutionary Guards Corps (IRGC) of Iran. However, this was playing both into Putin's and Assad's hands: not only were the insurgency and civic authorities their primary targets, but they declared both to be 'US-supported terrorists' and acted correspondingly. In turn, the Kremlin's propaganda machinery demonstratively declared the entire operation to be a 'high-precision' enterprise, and a 'war against terrorism' – indeed: as a war against the so-called 'Islamic State' (Daesh or IS, also known as ISIS/ISIL/IGIL): actually, only a mere handful of strikes by precision guided munition (PGM) were undertaken; even less so against the areas controlled by the IS, and it remains doubtful if even the GRU could ever explain what exactly was targeted there. After six months of up to 140 air strikes flown every day, the net result was minimal in military terms, but maximal in political terms. Contrary to the impressions created by Putin's propaganda, and although the VKS aviation group deployed at Hmeimim included modern types like the Su-30SM, Su-34, and, later on, Su-35, the mass of air strikes – over 80 percent – was flown by old Sukhoi Su-24M fighter-bombers. Regardless of whether old or newly acquired types, all the Russian fighter-bombers were deploying old, unguided bombs from the stocks built-up during the times of the USSR. Between 40 and 50 percent of Kh-101 and Kh-555 cruise missiles released by Tupolev Tu-95 and Tu-160 strategic bombers failed upon release or missed their targets. However, with the West's preoccupation with appeasing Putin in exchange for exporting commodities to Russia and importing cheap gas and oil, the native Syrian insurgency was isolated on the international scene, while millions of civilians fled into Turkey from where they began streaming into the European Union, destabilising the latter. Without the backing of the local population, the insurgency became overdependent on support from its foreign sponsors, mainly Turkey and Qatar, which in turn found themselves exposed to severe Russian pressure. Satisfied with the results, in February 2016 Putin declared the operation as completed and officially announced a withdrawal of the VSRF from Syria.

Although henceforth ignored by the Kremlin's propaganda machinery, the war actually went on: while the insurgency remained undefeated, Putin merely rotated troops and aircraft in and out of the country, and the IRGC insisted on imposing the Assadist regime in control over the whole of Syria. Through the summer and autumn of 2016, the VSRF and the IRGC thus focused their efforts upon forcing the insurgents out of Aleppo. Combined with the mass of Russian bombs, repeated Assadist attacks with chemical weapons not only massacred thousands, but caused another million to flee over the border and into Turkey. Once again, as soon as the battle was over, Putin announced an end of Russian involvement and withdrawal – and, once again, the fighting went on. Indeed, in spring 2017, insurgents launched an offensive against militias loyal to Assad, almost reaching the provincial capital Hama in the process. This time, it was a vicious and sustained aerial offensive by the VKS that forced them back into Idlib province, even though Putin's fliers continued deploying only obsolete free-fall bombs and unguided rockets. The fact was that due to their international isolation, the insurgency could not obtain any kind of effective anti-aircraft defence systems nor sustain the battle of attrition.

While Moscow was carrying out a fierce propaganda campaign emphasising the advanced equipment of the Russian group of forces in Syria, aiming to impress Western observers, in reality, over 50 percent of combat sorties flown by the VKS were undertaken by obsolete Sukhoi Su-24M tactical bombers. Up to 95–97 percent of combat sorties involved deployment of free-fall, or 'dumb', munitions. Even the number of upgraded Su-24M2s and Su-24M-SVP-24s remained very limited. (Russian MOD)

Finally, in November 2017, Putin announced an end to the military intervention and the withdrawal of the involved VSRF forces for the third time. However, the insurgency, the Assad regime, and the IRGC continued fighting, which is why VSK aircraft and the troops of at least a few Russian PMCs remain involved in the country five years later.

Cynical Triumph

Putin's military intervention in Syria thus remained not only a gamble on the international level but turned out to be a cynical triumph. Arguably, the insurgency was subdued – primarily because over 70 percent of the population was either converted into so-called 'internally displaced persons', inside Syria, or, and more often, forced to flee abroad. Essentially, the Russians thus helped Assad literally get rid of the majority of the Sunny Arab population of the country. However, what the Kremlin's propaganda machinery presented as a high-tech operation run in the style of NATO, and thus demonstrating that the Russian armed forces could match the same, was no such thing. Although up to 80 percent of VKS and VSRF personnel had rotated through the country over the preceding seven years (at least according to claims by the Ministry of Defence in Moscow), with few exceptions, they received next to no serious combat experience. Moreover, it remains doubtful that the GenStab drew any kind of useful lessons from this conflict; for example from the fact that the Syrian insurgents quickly learned to evade massive artillery barrages of the VSRF; or that makeshift UAVs deployed by the insurgency proved problematic to shoot down with the latest short-range surface-to-air missile systems (SAMs) of Russian origin, such as the Pantsyr S1 (ASCC/NATO-codename 'SA-22 Greyhound'), Tor M1 ('SA-15 Gauntlet'), or Buk ('SA-11 Gadfly'). Even publications in the specialised Russian military press indicated that the GenStab tended to ignore negative experiences with heavier SAMs – like those of the S-300 family (ASCC/NATO-codenames 'SA-10 Grumble' and 'SA-12 Gladiator/Giant') – which were positioned low near the coast, early on, and, in April 2018, failed to detect 50 RGM-109 Tomahawk Land Attack (TLAM-D) cruise missiles, launched by warships of the US Navy in retaliation for another chemical weapons attack by the Assadist regime. Lacking other solutions, in both cases the Russians merely increased the number of SAM systems deployed to protect their bases in Syria. However, the Syrian experience did have one profound change in the way Moscow conducted its expeditionary operations. Although the VSRF managed to keep its own casualties to the bare minimum (only about 40 cases of Russian servicemen killed in combat became known), starting in 2017, it began deploying PMCs as its primary tool of ground operations instead of the so-called *kontraktniki* (a topic that is will be discussed further below).

To Putin this mattered little, for thanks to the outright apathy of the West, he proved capable of winning his gamble: he conducted what was presented as a 'highly effective' military operation and scored a semblance of victory at a minimal price. Combined with the success in the Donbass of 2014–2015, the intervention in Syria thus appeared to demonstrate a significant improvement in the VSRF's capabilities. Indeed, the two operations impressed the mass of Western experts to the degree where they expected the Russians to have an easy game in Ukraine, should the war there ever conflagrate again.[12]

Chain of Command

Nominally at least, the chain of command of the Russian armed forces in 2022 was simple. President Vladimir Putin acted was the Supreme Commander-in-Chief of the Armed Forces, and issued his orders to the Minister of Defence, Sergei Shoygu, who had the authority over the GenStab – the chief of which, since 2012: Army General Valery Gerasimov – was selected by the president. That said, despite all the reforms under Serdyukov (or because of their reversals under Shoygu), the GenStab retained its composition, influence and crucial functions. Historically modelled after the Prussian *Großer Generalstab*, the body was staffed by a caste of professional planners that wore their own insignia, were never rotated through joint assignments, and thus never 'fixed' to a specific branch of arms. This was of particular importance because the GenStab had far wider authority and functions than, for example, its US equivalent – the Joint Chiefs of Staff – while suffering from far less 'branch fixation'. Although having no operational control of the force, it was responsible for:

- military intelligence (through the GRU)
- planning at operational and strategic levels (through its Main Operations Directorate)
- development of doctrine and capability, their standardisation and control of application of these (through its inspectors)

- procurement authority (through its Military Scientific Committee).[13]

Ironically, despite all the recent combat experience, the primary origin of the GenStab's doctrinal thinking of the early 2020s remained the Second World War: related experience had been studied for decades by literally millions of Soviet and then Russian military officers. Experience from the Afghanistan War of the 1980s, and Chechnya of the 1990s prompted some of the reforms described above, but in overall, the GenStab continued preparing the VSRF to fight the most intensive form of warfare imaginable to the Russians: a large-scale, conventional war under nuclear-threat conditions, and that based on lessons from over 70 years earlier. This is even more ironic considering that the officers assigned to the GenStab were hand-picked for their excellence early on in their career and underwent specialised training at the prestigious GenStab Academy – before spending their entire professional life doing staff work, but never exercised field command. As a result, members of this body formed a virtual 'cast' of supposed 'super-brains': officers meant to be specialised and to possess superior understanding of the science of war, capable of predicting how future wars were to be fought, and thus wrote all training manuals and oversaw the acquisition of all equipment (literally, from screws and spades to intercontinental ballistic missiles), the work of the three major branches and two independent corps of armed forces, all four strategic operations commands, and a miscellany of special units (like those responsible for railways and health) of the VSRF. As of 2017–2022, these branches were as follows:

- Ground Troops (*Sukhoputnyje voyska*; SV)
- Air-space Forces (*Vozdushno-kosmicheskiye sily*, VKS)
- Navy (*Voyenno-morskoy flot*; VMF)
- Strategic Rocket Troops (*Raketnye voyska strategicheskogo naznacheniya*; RVSN; including 60,000 troops in 12 missile divisions, operating 299 fixed and mobile intercontinental ballistic missiles with 1,200 nuclear warheads)
- Airborne Troops (*Vozdushno-desantny Voyska*, VDV; essentially a rapid reaction force with special operations capability)

While the GenStab determined the doctrine and equipment, the SV, VKS, and the VMF were all responsible for administering their forces, only: all the operational control was exercised by OSKs (within their geographic areas of responsibility) – the work of which was controlled by the President, Minister of Defence and the Chief of the GenStab – from the National Defence Management Centre (*Natsionalnyi tsentr upravlenya oboronoy*, NtsUO), operational since 2014.[14]

Manpower of the VSRF[15]

One of the biggest uncertainties for foreign observers attempting to assess the capabilities of the VSRF through the early twenty-first century was its manpower: the number of officers and other ranks actually in service. There were a number of factors to be taken into consideration, the first of which was the huge number of officers, the second the continuous shortfalls in regards of recruitment of other ranks, and the third lay in massive differences between the MODs and GenStab's wishes, planning and reality.

On paper, the total manpower of the VSRF was never fewer than one million troops. Indeed, for most of the period between 1990 and 2010, the nominal headcounts varied at between 1.2 and 1.7 million. However, socio-economic factors resulted in massive shortfalls. By 2016, when the nominal number was reduced to one million, the real number was down to 770,000: repeated efforts to increase the real number ever since have all failed.

In addition to lacking troops – primarily soldiers and NCOs – the VSRF was short of junior officers; specialists in charge of maintenance of its construction, equipment, finances, vehicles, and military infrastructure, all of which in turn meant that even if the MOD and the GenStab could find enough recruits, and equip them suitably, they could not expand the total force for the lack of capability to command, control and support it. The net result of this was that the VSRF was capable of deploying only about 250,000 ground troops for the invasion of Ukraine; that its logistics struggled when this many were involved in combat operations; and that it would continue experiencing similar problems for a while longer: indeed, that despite much-publicised mobilisations initiated in September 2022, the Russian armed forces faced a continuous decline in the total number of troops they were capable of deploying to the frontlines in Ukraine.

Table 6: Branches of the VSRF and their Manpower as of 2019

Branch or Corps	Designation	Manpower
SV	*Sukhoputnyje voyska*, Ground troops	280,000
VDV	*Vozdushno-desantnye voyska*, Airborne troops	45,000
VKS	*Vozdushno-kosmicheskiye sily*, Aerospace Forces	165,000
VMF	*Voyenno-morskoy flot*, Navy	150,000

Ground Forces

While the VDV and the Navy controlled some ground units and special operation forces, by far the biggest part of the VSRF remained the SV (Ground Forces), the major units of which were divisions and brigades.[16] Nominally, each of the nine motor rifle divisions extant as of 2019–2022, had two motor rifle regiments, and a regiment each of tanks, artillery, and anti-aircraft defences, plus a battalion each of engineers, reconnaissance, signals, anti-tank weapons, and logistic support. All were concentrated in western Russia and carried the designations of traditional units from earlier times. The only two tank divisions were organised in a similar fashion, but had two tank regiments and one motor rifle regiment. There were 21 motorised rifle brigades as of 2021, each of which included three motor rifle battalions and a single tank battalion.

In reality, each brigade and division had between three and six battalion tactical groups ready for combat operations: these were subordinated to combined arms armies, tank armies, or army corps depending on the task, and complemented by an array of supporting units, like those specialised for command purposes, artillery, anti-aircraft, missile, or logistics. Because of this, the nominal strength of brigades and divisions did not matter: what did matter was that every BTG of a motor rifle division, brigade, or regiment was centred on a motor rifle battalion including two or three rifle companies, with three platoons each, sometimes reinforced by a battery of 120mm mortars – all mounted either on BMP-2, BMP-3 or BTR-82 IFVs, or MT-LB APCs. Even then, the total strength of each BTG varied significantly because BMP-equipped units required no additional anti-tank elements, as usually attached to units operating the more lightly armed BTRs or MT-LBs. The tank element of every BTG

A pre-war photograph of a T-72 MBT and a BTR-80 APC of the 126th Coastal Defence Brigade of the VSRF. This unit was to play an important role in the Russian advance on Kherson, Mykolaiv, and beyond. (Russian MOD)

usually included only a company of 10 tanks, organised into three platoons of three, and one command tank. BTGs drawn from tank divisions or regiments, included two or three companies of 10 MBTs each, and similar support elements to motor rifle BTGs. Regardless of whether tank or motor rifle, every BTG included a battery each of self-propelled guns and multiple rocket launchers, a battery of air defence missiles, a company of engineers, and at least a platoon each of electronic warfare, reconnaissance, signals, maintenance and medical troops. The primary combat units of the SV/VSRF as of 2014 are listed in Appendix II.

Putin's Little Green Men: Spetsnaz, VDV and Naval Infantry

Perhaps the most important element of the VSRF during the invasion of Ukraine in 2014, and certainly one of the most important during the aggression of 2022, were the so-called Spetsnaz troops.[17] Subordinated directly to the GRU, and staffed exclusively by the professionals, the Spetsnaz were organised into one 1,500-strong brigade (the 45th), and nine slightly smaller but specialised units (2nd, 3rd Guards, 10th, 14th, 16th, 24th Guards, 100th and 346th Brigades) – of which one (the 346th) was assigned to the Special Forces Command. Most of the Spetsnaz were trained for infiltration and long-range reconnaissance tasks, but many received training in commando operations. Gauging by media reports released after 24 February 2022, more than a dozen Spetsnaz teams infiltrated Ukraine days before the aggression, with the aim of identifying key targets and attacking them, assassinating members of government and local authorities, and conducting sabotage and diversion operations.

Nominally trained for any mission in all terrain and climates, the airborne assault units – abbreviated in Russian as VDV – were the spearhead of the Russian armed forces: the first troops to be employed in any major crisis or conflict. Holding an elite status and including the highest proportion of the *kontraktniki*, the VDV troops always received the cream of the conscripts. Equipped with armoured vehicles designed to be air transportable, but still trained as a mechanised force, they served both as a politically reliable rapid reaction force, and a mobile force capable of conducting operations in the enemy's depth. As of 2020, they were organised into three airborne divisions and an air assault division (each of roughly 5,500 men), and three air assault brigades. Each division had either two or three parachute or air assault regiments, an air defence and an artillery regiment each, and reconnaissance, engineer, and logistics battalions. In turn, each air assault regiment comprised three airborne or air assault battalions, an artillery battalion, reconnaissance, signals, engineering, and tank companies, and a battery each of anti-tank and air defence weapons. Overall, the entire VDV had about 45,000 troops and at least 2,300 armoured vehicles, organised into 43 battalions.[18]

Another sub-branch of the VSRF frequently described as 'elite', was the Naval Infantry. Administered by the Navy and specialised in amphibious operations, the majority of such units were organised into brigades of about 2,500 troops each, the equipment of which differed significantly: five brigades (61st of the Northern Fleet, the 336th of the Baltic Fleet, the 810th of the Black Sea Fleet, and the 40th and the 155th of the Pacific Fleet) included a dedicated airborne assault battalion and a tank company, and all were equipped with a combination of BTR-82 IFVs, and upgraded T-72 and T-80 MBTs.[19]

Table 7: VDV Units of the VSRF, 2021

Unit	Notes
7th Guards Airborne Division	6th Air Assault, 108th Air Assault, 247th Air Assault, 1141st Artillery regiments
76th Guards Airborne Division	104th Air Assault, 234th Air Assault and 237th Air Assault, 1140th Artillery regiments
98th Guards Airborne Division	217th Airborne, 331st Airborne, 1065th Artillery regiments
106th Guards Airborne Division	51st Airborne, 137th Airborne, 1182nd Artillery regiments
11th Guards Air Assault Brigade	
31st Guards Air Assault Brigade	
83rd Guards Air Assault Brigade	
45th Guards Spetsnaz Brigade	

Putin's 'God of War': Artillery

While traditionally Soviet, and subsequently Russian, airborne troops, tanks and IFVs have attracted most attention from foreign observers – and although even the Soviet and Russian military theoreticians insisted that the best weapon against a tank is another tank – the centrepiece of the VSRF's doctrine, whether for a large-scale conventional war or counterinsurgency warfare, was always artillery. Based on concepts developed in the 1920s and 1930s, and perfected during the Second World War (when their artillery broke the back of both the Wehrmacht on the Eastern Front, and the Japanese Kwantung Army in Manchuria), Soviet and Russian formations have always been equipped with very large quantities of artillery. The reason was that the GenStab's theoreticians insisted that without effective suppression of the defender's anti-tank weapons, no high-speed advance could succeed. For the suppression of lines of fortifications in the path of the advancing troops, they preferred a complex, rolling barrage: alternatively, when the defence was organised on a belt of strong points, they wanted to engage each with massive volumes of concentrated fire. With Soviet air power traditionally proving unable to deliver a comparable tonnage of high explosives with the necessary precision, the artillery became their preferred tool. Following exactly the same principles, the theoreticians of the VSRF GenStab built-up artillery for a combination of firepower and manoeuvrability: by 2022, more than half of it was self-propelled.

The spearhead of the VSRF's artillery were missile units equipped with 9K720 Iskander ballistic missiles (ASCC/NATO-codename 'SS-26 Stone'). Developed in the late 1990s, Iskander is a road-mobile system designed to fire single-stage, inertially guided missiles weighing around 3,800kg, against point and area targets such as command posts, communication nodes, or troops in concentration areas. Carrying either a high-explosive fragmentation or submunition warhead weighing (depending on type) between 480 and 700kg, it could reach targets around 400km distant, and had a circular error probable (CEP) of 20–30 metres.[20] The much improved and hypersonic-capable variant, the 9M723K1 Iskander-M was a single-stage, so-called 'quasi ballistic' missile, that could perform evasive manoeuvres in the terminal phase of flight and release decoys to improve its capability to penetrate missile defence systems. Weighing 4,615kg, the Iskander-M included an electro-optical seeker head and was controlled throughout the

A transporter-erector-launcher (TEL) of the Iskander system of the VSRF, shown in the process of raising the missile into a firing position. (Ukrainian MOD)

In addition to four brigades of Iskander-M ballistic missiles, as of 2022, the VSRF operated two sub-variants of this system equipped with six different types of other missiles. Amongst these were 9M728 (also known as R-500) and 9M729 cruise missiles of the Iskander-K system, a TEL of which is shown here. (Russian MOD)

entire flight, enabling it a pinpoint accuracy (CEP of 5–7m) over a range of about 415km. As of 2022, the VSRF operated about 160 firing units organised into 13 brigades.

While Iskanders were to play an important role in striking concentrations of Ukrainian forces during the first few months of the invasion, the actual centrepiece of the SV/VFRS were units operating conventional tube artillery and artillery rockets, primarily those equipped with about 200 BM-27 Uragan 220mm multiple rocket launchers, around 100 BM-30 Smerch 300mm MRLS, and about 20 9A52-4 Tornado-S systems (an upgrade of the Smerch). Such units included a strong UAV component, equipped with highly flexible, even if small, short ranged, and primitive Orlan-10s. Rocket artillery brigades were usually smaller than those operating heavy tube artillery: with a strength of about 1,000 personnel, these were comparable in size to artillery groups of motor rifle brigades. Most

The heaviest and longest-ranged multiple rocket launch system in service with the VSRF as of 2022 was the BM-30 Smerch, equipped with twelve 300mm tubes for a variety of artillery rockets capable of reaching ranges between 120 and 200km. (Russian MOD)

A 2S7 Pion – the heaviest self-propelled howitzer (203mm calibre) the VSRF deployed in Ukraine in 2022 – seen underway towards the Ukrainian border in the Belgorod area in early 2022. (Russian Internet)

comprised two divisions of MSTA-S self-propelled 152mm guns, or 2S7 Pion/2S7A Malka 203mm self-propelled guns – usually complemented by a division of MRLS and an anti-tank division. In addition to about 400–500 MSTA-S, the SV/VSRF operated between 500 and 700 similar, yet smaller and shorter-ranged 2S3 Akatsiya self-propelled howitzers, and several hundreds of towed D-20, 2A65 MSTA-B, and 2A36 Giatsint-B 152mm artillery pieces. Over 500 older and lighter 122mm artillery pieces – such as the 2S1 Gvozdika and 2S34 Hosta – were still in service, as were about 40 2S4 Tyulpan self-propelled 240mm mortars.

All the artillery units were networked with Orlan UAVs with help of the USS TZ computer application that served as an ATMS, enabling artillery commanders to monitor the work of the UAV in real time, and coordinate fire operations with a very quick reaction time.[21]

Putin's Pasdaran: Rosgvardiya and OMON[23]

Because of the constant shortfalls of troops for the VSRF, and unlike 2014, as of 2022 the VSRF was far from exercising even administrative control over all the uniformed and armed formations existent in Russia. On the contrary, the Kremlin controlled several highly militarised organisations tasked with internal security. The oldest amongst them was the Border Guard service, but the biggest and most powerful was the Federal National Guard Service (*Federalnaya sluzhba Voysk Natsionalnoy gvardii Rossiyskoy Federatsii*, usually abbreviated to Rosgvardia). Established in 2016 and headquartered in Moscow, this was still a relatively new service, but already about 340,000 strong. Commanded by Viktor Zolotov (Putin's chief bodyguard), and responsible solely to the president, the Rosgvardia was primarily tasked with securing the government against what Moscow defined as 'hybrid warfare': essentially against the 'colour' revolutions that toppled several of Putin's allies in Europe and elsewhere since 1999. Correspondingly, it was equipped and trained to quell protests, protect vital infrastructure, and coordinate the wide array of private or public security corporations. That said, the Rosgvardia already had elements trained in counterterrorism and counterinsurgency operations, and several larger units organised and trained to support the VSRF in rear areas. The service was organised into eight territorial districts, corresponding to the federal districts of Russia:

- Central (HQ Moscow)
- Northwestern (HQ Saint Petersburg)
- North Caucasian (HQ Pyatitgorsk)
- Southern (HQ Rostov-na-Donu)
- Volga (HQ Nizhny Novgorod)

Spetsnaz troops of the Rosgvardia seen during a pre-war parade. (Kremlin.ru)

- Ural (HQ Yekaterinenburg)
- Siberian (HQ Novosibirsk)
- Eastern (HQ Khabarovsk)

The majority of Rosgvardia's servicemen were little more than de-facto police: overweight volunteers with little training and lightly armed, serving as guards at selected points around the country. However, operational forces of this branch (*Operativnogo naznacheniya*, ON) included its biggest unit, the 10,000-strong Dzerzhinsky Spetsnaz Division in Moscow; 16 detachments comprising another 10,000 Spetsnaz troops were distributed around the country; 12 Spetsnaz brigades and several regiments (all trained in counterinsurgency operations and equipped with BTR APCs). Perhaps the most notorious amongst them was the 'Kadyrovtsy', the loyalists of Ramazan Kadyrov, President of the Chechen Republic and one of Putin's closest allies: the official designation of this unit was the 141st Special Motorised Regiment Akhmat-Khadzi Kadyrov. Atop of this, the Rosgvardia had its own air arm, operating about 100 Mi-8s, 10 Mi-26s, at least eight Mi-24s, and a dozen Ansat and Ka-226 helicopters, 10 Il-76 and 10 An-26 transports, and a fleet of small UAVs of different types.

A Russian orthodox priest blessing new assault rifles of the OMON, in Stavropol in early 2022. (OMON)

Another important branch responsible for internal security was the OMON, which is the Russian abbreviation for 'Mobile Detachments of Special Purpose' (*Otriad mobilny ossobogo naznacheniya*). Generally, there were two types of OMON units: one, designated the Special Units for Rapid Reaction (*Spetsialnye otryady bystrigo reagirovanya*, SOBR) included about 40,000 troops organised into 160 detachments, amongst them a few hundred of Kadyrov's Chechens and about 12,000 operators trained in combating organised crime and terrorism. Another 40,000 troops were assigned to the Guards Units (*Voyska okhranyy goroda*, VOG), dedicated to the protection of critical infrastructure.

Putin's discrete Mobilisation: Private Military Companies and the BARS

Due to the lack of funding, during the 1990s and 2000s, the VSRF ceased the practice of recalling reservists. In turn, it continued experiencing shortages of ground troops. Therefore, Putin and the Ministry of Defence began seeking for ways to create a trained reserve in a cheaper fashion. A working solution emerged only in 2011–2012, when Putin created a legal background for the MOD to sponsor military training for members of the – reportedly –

Ramazan Kadyrov (right), one of Putin's closest allies, seen in his typical pose – wearing Prada-designed boots with a price tag of about €1,100. (Kremlin.ru)

PUTIN'S LITTLE EAGLE AND ARTILLERY APP: ORLAN-10 AND THE UNIFIED TACTICAL CONTROL SYSTEM

Developed by the Special Technology Centre (STC) in Saint Petersburg, the Orlan-10 featured a composite hull that reduced its radar signature. This was also its only part manufactured in Russia: the rest of the UAV – including the engine, electronics, cameras, GPS module and all other components – was made of easily acquirable commercial electronic components, widely available in Russia despite Western sanctions.

Orlan-10s were usually deployed in trios:

- One was always equipped with a camera and usually operated at altitudes of 1,000–1,500 metres. By May 2022, the Ukrainians had identified at least seven different camera systems installed into Orlans, including Canon EOS 750D/EOS 800D digital cameras (with an EF 85mm f/1.8 USM lens) and Lynred PIC0640gen2 infrared or TM2005016-F19 thermal cameras. By 2022, an upgraded version had become available, comprising a laser designator in addition to the camera, enabling the Orlan-10 to mark targets for precision guided shells like Krasnopol.
- The second Orlan-10 usually carried a SIGINT package, such as the Leer-3 system, capable of faking a GSM station in order to detect and track mobile telephones using GSM systems, and also radio stations and radar systems (the same Leer-3 was – together with Windows 7 – used as the control interface for the Orlan-10).
- The third Orlan-10 served as an airborne relay for the first two: forwarding control inputs to them, and constantly receiving the collected intelligence from them, and forwarding this to the base.

A pair of such trios proved capable of detecting and tracking down almost all sources of radio waves and providing heatmaps denoting their concentrations to their operators.

The core of the high effectiveness of the Orlan-10 was its highly flexible software – which enabled the UAV to remain operational regardless of what kind of components were installed. Another important element was the software connecting it to artillery units: the Unified System for Managing a Tactical Unit (Единая система управления тактического звена, ЕСУ ТЗ, or, simplified, Unified Tactical Control System, UTCS). Developed following the failure of the first Russian digital ATMS, Metronome, tested in Syria in 2015–2016, the primary purpose of the UTCS was communication between UAVs, forward artillery observers, and artillery. With it, both the UAV operator and the forward artillery observer (FAO, also known in the West as 'Joint Tactical Air/Artillery Controller', JTAC) could pinpoint detected enemy positions on their tablets, and forward their coordinates to artillery in real time, with minimal delay.[22]

Certainly enough, the Russians never had enough Orlan-10s to cover more than relatively limited sectors of the LOC in eastern Ukraine, and these were unable to operate at more than a few kilometres behind the enemy frontline. Moreover, for the first two months of their aggression of 2022, the weather was cold and wet, and Orlan-10s were limited to operations at temperatures above 5°C. Similarly, the SV was chronically short of FAOs and modern equipment for them. Consequently, both FAOs and Orlans were a rare sight early

A serviceman of the VSRF preparing an Orlan-10 UAV for launch from a catapult. (Russian MOD)

600,000-strong Russian Cossacks Association. This in turn gave birth to the idea of establishing mercenary assets – a discipline in which tsarist Russia had long traditions. The first of the private military companies (PMCs), the little-known Alpha Group, had been in existence since around 2008 and hired former operatives of the GRU. By 2011, it was followed by the PMCs Antiterror, Moran Security Group, and Redut-Antiterror. Moran was hiring from the FSB and Navy personnel, while Redut became closely associated with the 45th Spetsnaz Brigade. In turn, Moran gave birth to the Slavonic Corps, established upon request from the Assad regime in 2013 and then reorganised as Wagner, a year later. Owned by Yevgeny Prigozhin (Putin's former cook) but led by Dmitriy Utkin (a declared neo-Nazi and former member of Moran), the Molkino-based Wagner was originally staffed by members of the 2nd Spetsnaz Brigade, GRU.

Initially at least, all the PMCs were mainly hiring demobilised troops from units disbanded by Serdyukov's reforms. However, their very existence was against the law, and the top ranks of the FSB, GRU, and the GenStab opposed their existence for a combination of commercial and ideological interests. However, Putin favoured this solution for his own reasons: they offered him another opportunity for 'shareholding' (channelling public money into his pockets and those of his favourites through contracting PMCs), and it created an additional armed force to counter any kind of disloyalty –

during the war. This caused many complaints either about completely ineffective artillery barrages – even if an hour long – or about infantry being sent into 'human wave' style attacks without any kind of air and/or artillery support (indeed, even without platoon leaders and very few company commanders). Thus, the few FAOs and Orlan-10s that saw action primarily did so in the south, where local ambient temperatures were high enough.

In turn, although knowing details of the VSRF's reconnaissance-fire system, and having shot down about a dozen Orlan-10s since 2014, the Ukrainians underwent a protracted process of learning-by-doing while trying to counter them – before realising that this task required a defence system on its own. The easiest way of countering Orlan-10s was to jam the GPS guidance signals: while knowing how to do this, they had too little of the necessary equipment. Alternatively, one could shoot down the Orlan-10s: MANPADs like the British-made Martlet and Starstreak, US FIM-92 Stinger, or the Soviet/Russian/Ukrainian-made Strelas have all proven effective against them.

An Orlan-10 uses a parachute to aid its recovery following a reconnaissance flight. (Russian MOD)

A MSTA-S self-propelled 152mm howitzer on the move in eastern Ukraine during early March 2022. (Russian MOD)

However, they were available in limited numbers, while expensive and short ranged, and thus unable to cover the entire battlefield whenever necessary. The third way of countering Orlan-10s was that of shooting them down with guns. The Ukrainians are known to have deployed Browning M2 .50/12.7mm machine guns, and 20mm, 23mm, and 30mm light anti-aircraft guns. However, the Russians then began operating their UAVs at slightly higher altitudes, rendering all of these ineffective. Moreover, teams operating MANPADs and other light antiaircraft weapons were frequently disrupted by the combination they were supposed to counter: Orlan-10 UAVs and MSTA-S howitzers, connected by the UTCS application.

especially from within the VSRF. Finally, he found it opportune to keep thousands of demobilised troops 'busy and happy while serving', rather than letting them create instability inside Russia. Perhaps unsurprisingly, in 2016, he assigned the task of controlling and coordinating all the PMCs to the Rosgvardia. Outside the country, PMCs not only offered the option of deploying military force in situations where the Russian population might be sensitive to casualties, but plausible deniability, too. Therefore, through 2014–2018, Wagner was tasked with supporting the Separatists in the Donbass and then the Assad regime, and, as it continued to grow, also saw deployments in Libya, Sudan, Mali, and the Central African Republic, where it earned itself a notorious reputation.

However, as already mentioned, the sheer existence of PMCs was against the law in the Russian Federation. Moreover, the top ranks of the FSB, GRU, and the GenStab were all left outside the group of those profiting from them, and Prigzohin was at odds with both Shoygu and the Ministry of Defence. Unsurprisingly, all three bodies remained strictly against the PMCs and took care that they were never to be legalised by the Duma (the Russian Parliament). Ultimately, this became the reason why next to no PMCs became involved in the early operations against Ukraine in 2022 – with one exception: Redut-Antiterror. Organised into five small battalions (each some 150–200 strong and designated Axes, Hooligans, Ilimovtsy, Marines, and Wolves), the latter intensified hiring mercenaries – all former members of the 45th Spetsnaz Brigade – for an operation in the Donbass in mid-December 2021, and is known to have started deploying them for long-range reconnaissance deep inside Ukraine in mid-February 2022. During preparations for the assault on Kyiv, Redut-Antiterror created an additional but smaller detachment, designated North, this was assigned to the 45th Spetsnaz Brigade, together with a detachment of another new creation that came into being in the meantime.

Continuing to experience shortages of ground troops, in 2020–2021, the MOD joined the practice of hiring from the ranks of demobilised servicemen through establishing the Combat Army Reserve of the Country (abbreviated in Russian as BARS). BARS sought to keep those Russians who had just concluded their national service in 'prepared mobilisation state' through sending them on additional training courses. By 2022, it had established more than 20 regiments (the mass of them drafted within the Southern Military District), several of which took part in large-scale exercises: one BARS unit, the Ivanovo Detachment, was also assigned to the 45th Spetsnaz Brigade's assault on Kyiv.[24]

Putin's Red Stars

As of early 2022, the Russian Aerospace Forces (*Vozdushno-kosmicheskiye sily*; VKS) comprised three main branches:

- Air Force (*Voyenno-vozdushnye sily*; VVS)
- Air Defence and Missile Troops (*Voyska protivovozdushnoy I protivoraketnoy oborony*)
- Space Troops (*Kosmicheskie voyska*)

The VVS, administratively responsible for all the aircraft and the mass of helicopters, was composed of seven main entities: four air force and air defence armies (one for each of the OSKs, and including ground-based air defence assets), the Long Range Aviation (*Dalnyaya aviatsiya*; DA), the Military Transport Aviation (*Voyenno-transportnaya aviatsiya*, VTA), and units answering directly to the VKS headquarters (including the Special Purpose Aviation Division with more than 100 aircraft mostly tasked with VIP transport duties; the Composite Aviation Group in Syria; various test and research centres, the training facilities and schools, and the 185th Combat Training and Combat Application Centre, which included an Aggressor Squadron equipped with old MiG-29SMT fighter-bombers). The Navy also had its own aviation (*Morskaya aviatsiya Voenno-morskogo flota*, MA VMF), administratively responsible for an array of units attached to its different fleets, but subjected to the operational control of the OSKs.

Organisationally, the VKS was structured into air defence divisions, each of which controlled several air defence regiments equipped with S-300, S-400, Buk and Pantsir-S systems (with the latter two systems primarily tasked with point defence protection of the first two).

Small groups of the FSB, GRU, Spetsnaz, and members of the Redut PMC were amongst the first Russian forces to be clandestinely infiltrated into Ukraine in mid-February 2022, with the task of conducting reconnaissance. (Russian MOD)

A Su-34 tactical bomber (serial RF-93838) of the 559th Bomber Aviation Regiment (BAP), seen during an exercise in 2019. (Photo by Daniele Faccioli)

A front view of a Mi-28 helicopter of the VKS (serial RF-95315), seen at Kubinka AB in 2019, armed with a B-8M pod for unguided rockets. Notable is the turret with Shipunov 2A42 30mm automatic cannon. (Photo by Daniele Faccioli)

Most aircraft and helicopters were operated by regiments – the types of which are detailed in Table 8 – each of which included two or three squadrons with 8 to 12 aircraft, for a total of 24–26 machines, 350–450 officers and 900–1,200 other ranks. Bomber and transport regiments had smaller squadrons of 8–10 aircraft each, and a complement of 350–450 personnel. Helicopter regiments had two or three squadrons of 12–16 helicopters, of which one was usually equipped with attack types and two with transport or assault types. Overall, as of late 2018, the VVS and the MA VMF operated a total of about 1,000 tactical combat aircraft, 485 transports, 126 bombers, 375 attack and 348 assault/transport helicopters, and another 130 reconnaissance and electronic warfare aircraft.

Nominally, both services benefitted from extensive modernisation carried out through the 2010s, which enabled the replacement of the large part of their fighter-bomber and helicopter fleets. For example, the heavy bomber fleet – meanwhile entirely integrated into the DA of the VKS – was overhauled and significantly upgraded; Sukhoi Su-34 tactical bombers replaced a large part of the obsolescent Sukhoi Su-24M fleet, while many of the latter were upgraded to the Su-24M2 and Su-24M SVP-24 standard. Over 300 newly-built Su-30M2s, Su-30SMs, and Su-35Ss took over from old MiG-29s; and a large part of the Su-27 fleet was overhauled and upgraded to the Su-27SM standard. That said, MiG-31 interceptors and Su-25 attack aircraft were not replaced: only overhauled and upgraded to MiG-31BM and Su-25SM3 standards, respectively. Both services took care to overhaul their helicopter fleets: the majority of remaining Mil Mi-24s were replaced by modern Ka-52s, Mil Mi-35s and Mi-28Ns, and hundreds of new Mi-8s were also acquired.

At least nominally, both the newly acquired and upgraded older aircraft were roughly comparable to the so-called '4th Generation' of fighter-bombers of Western origin, such as the Boeing F-15 or Lockheed-Martin F-16. Indeed, the Su-35S was often assessed as on a par with the Eurofighter EF-2000 Typhoon. However, because of the shortcomings of the Russian electronics industry, which lagged behind both its Western and Chinese counterparts – they all were plagued with inferior avionics and – especially – weapons systems: indeed, many of the new avionics systems on the 'best' of the Sukhoi-designed fighter-bombers included computers and even software of Western origin, while their replacement with 'made in Russia' equivalents – for example: Su-27SM3 and Su-30SM3 variants – were repeatedly delayed. Moreover, the VKS lacked so-called 'force multipliers' like airborne early warning and control (AWACS) aircraft, and tankers. Only 10 Beriev A-50s were still in service, some of them meanwhile upgraded to the A-50U standard; the work on a much-improved A-100 was delayed for years. Similarly, although all the Su-30s, Su-34s and Su-35s were equipped with in-flight refuelling systems, there were only 15 Ilyushin Il-78 tankers, and they were mainly tasked with supporting the DA's bombers.

Above all, all of the new aircraft were actually based on old designs, which entered service during the last decade of the USSR: the sole new combat aircraft design to enter flight-testing with the VKS became the Sukhoi Su-57. Nominally a 'stealth' fighter, this was not only plagued by protracted developmental issues and shortage of funding but delayed for decades, and its true operational status remained uncertain at best.

In similar fashion, the GenStab completely failed to renew the VKS's arsenal of guided weapons of all kinds. Arguably, the production of modern cruise missiles – mainly those of the Kh-101 family, deployed from Tu-160 and Tu-95MS bombers, and representing the principal long-range weapon of the VKS – was continued, but at low rate. Due to the loss of contact with the Ukrainian defence sector, production of precision guided munitions in Russia came to a standstill and had to be restarted from scratch: local factories managed to assemble about a dozen each of the newly designed weapons through the eight years up to 2022. Even production of the urgently needed, much-expected, and often famed R-37M and R-77-1 active-radar homing, long- and medium-range air-to-air missiles, respectively, started only in the 2016–2017 period, resulting in relatively low stocks. Thus, as of early 2022, the VKS went into the war largely armed with old free-fall bombs, air-to-air missiles already compromised by the West back in the 1980s, and a stock of PGMs left behind from the times of the USSR.

Table 8: VVS and VMF, Main Types of Regiments

BAP	*Bombardirovochnyi Aviapolk*; Bomber Aviation Regiment
Br AA	*Brigada Armeyskoy aviatsii*; Army Aviation Brigade
IAP	*Istrebitelnyi Aviapolk*; Fighter Aviation Regiment
KIAP	*Korabelnyi Istrebitelnyi Aviapolk*; Shipborne Fighter Aviation Regiment
MshAP	*Morskoy Shturmovoy Polk*; Naval Attack Aviation Regiment
SAP	*Smeshannyi Aviapolk*; Composite Aviation Regiment
ShAP	*Istrebitelno-shturmovaya aviapolk*; Attack Aviation Regiment
TBAP	*Tyazholy Bombardirovochnyi Aviapolk*; Heavy Bomber Aviation Regiment
VP	*Vertolonyi Polk*; Helicopter Regiment
VTAP	*Voyenno-transportny aviapolk*; Military Transport Aviation Regiment

Extended-Range Artillery[25]

If the poor state of the VKS's weapons for tactical aircraft was not enough, the status of its training was even worse. Contrary to impressions created by the Russian political and military elite over the previous 30 years, the GenStab continued to consider air power for little more than 'air defence' and 'extended-range artillery' and envisaged its role correspondingly. This in turn mean that except for heavy bombers of the DA, operational control over all the aircraft and helicopters of the VKS was in the hands of the OSKs, the headquarters of which were dominated by officers of the ground forces. In such atmosphere, and regardless of theoretical capabilities of its machinery, the Air Force was equipped and trained with the principal purpose of supporting ground troops and naval forces, up to a depth of perhaps 20–30km behind the front line: it was never meant to operate independently from the other branches of the VSRF, while the task of delivering strikes against the enemy depth was given to the units equipped with cruise-missile-carrying heavy bombers, and ballistic missiles. Interceptors of the VKS had two tasks: air defence in depth, and air superiority over the battlefield. Fighter-bombers were to strike geographic coordinates provided to their crews either before the flight, or by the A-50s while already airborne, but never to more than 5–20km behind the front line. Attack aircraft and helicopters were to operate directly over the battlefield – where at least the Mi-24s and Mi-35s were still deployed in, essentially, similar fashion to the attack aircraft, without hovering or ambushing enemy vehicles.

Furthermore, the training philosophy of the VKS remained conservative and driven by flight safety. Initial training of cadets took no less than five years, but they started flying only in their fourth year, while receiving only about 150 hours of basic training in flying combat aircraft during the last year. Once assigned to combat units, the pilots had to go through a very long, gradual process of improving their skills through repetitive exercises in simple navigation and operations around their base: the training system envisaged them taking eight years to develop all their skills to the maximum – and this in a situation where average pilot received only 80–100 hours of flying per year, often even fewer.

Overall, the VKS was designed, equipped and trained in a significantly different fashion than any NATO-style air force, or indeed, most other air forces around the world. Major VKS and VMF units as of 2018–2022 are detailed in Appendix III.

The Black Sea Fleet

Headquartered in occupied Sevastopol on the Crimea Peninsula, the Black Sea Fleet was in a sorry state as of the late 2000s, having received no new ships for 20 years. This situation experienced a fundamental change in 2014, when the recovery of the fleet received a priority: by early 2018, it received 50 new vessels, including:

- Project 636.3-class submarines *Novorossiysk, Rostov-na-Donu, Stary Oskol, Krasnodar, Velikiy Novgorod*, and *Kolpino*, in addition to the single Project 877V-class boat, *Alrosa*
- Project 11356M-class frigates *Admiral Grigorovich, Admiral Essen*, and *Admiral Makarov*
- Project 1135-class frigates *Pytlivy* and *Ladny*
- Project 21631 Buryan-M-class missile corvettes *Vyshniy, Volochvok, Orkehovo, Zuyevo, Ingushetiya*, and *Grayoron*
- Project 22800-class corvettes *Mytishchi* and *Tsiklok*
- Project 12700-class minesweepers *Ivan Antonov, Vladimir Emelyanov*, and *Georgy Kurbatov*
- numerous patrol boats, anti-sabotage boats
- Project 18280-class intelligence gathering ship *Ivan Khurs*

These ships reinforced the fleet's flagship, the 30-year-old guided missile cruiser *Moskva* – which was returned to semi-operational condition through an overhaul, but never modified: indeed, it seems that a large part of its weaponry was non-functional.

Another large segment of the Russian Navy to see at least some action in Ukraine, and early during the invasion, was the Caspian Sea Flotilla – which, like the Black Sea Fleet, was subordinated to the OSK South. During the 2010s, this was modernised through the addition of:

- Project 11661K-class frigates *Dagestan* and *Tatarstan*
- Project 21630-class missile corvettes *Astrakhan, Volgodonsk*, and *Mahachkala*
- Project 21631 Buryan-M-class missile corvettes *Grad Sviyazhsk, Uglich*, and *Velikiy Ustyug*

All of these ships were capable of reaching the Black Sea via the Volga-Don Canal and the Azov Sea. Most importantly, all the newly constructed frigates, corvettes and submarines were armed with 3M-54 Kalibr anti-ship missiles (ASCC/NATO-codename 'SS-N-27 Sizzler'), and 3M14K and 3M14T ('SS-N-30A') land-attack cruise missiles.

The Black Sea Fleet also received a strong amphibious component, including:

- Project 1171-class landing ships *Nikolay Filichenkov* and *Orsk*
- Project 775-class amphibious assault ships *Novocherkassk, Azov, Cesar Kunikov* and *Yamal*

Combined, these five vessels had the capacity to carry about 150 combat vehicles of the Naval Infantry.

The Black Sea Fleet saw significant action during the 2010s, including against Georgia (when two of its corvettes claimed the sinking of an enemy vessel), and especially during the intervention in Syria, when the 810th Naval Infantry Brigade spearheaded the deployment of Russian troops, amphibious assault and transport ships carried the mass of ammunition and supplies for VSRF troops, and warships and submarines (and several ships of the Caspian Sea Flotilla), fired multiple volleys of cruise missiles.

Another new aspect of the Russian naval strategy in the Black Sea – and one that became possible through the annexation of the Crimea – was the deployment of several S-300 and S-400 SAM systems, and at least one K-300P Bastion-P coastal defence missile system (ASCC/NATO-codename 'SS-C-5 Stooge'), equipped with supersonic P-800 Oniks dual-role anti-ship and land-attack missiles with a range of 120–300km, depending on the selected trajectory.[26]

Combined Arms Doctrine

As mentioned above, Soviet and then Russian officers had spent decades studying solely the lessons and statistics from what is known as the 'Great Patriotic War' in Russia, while largely ignoring experience from 'lesser' conflicts fought since 1945. The unsurprising result was their dogmatic indoctrination, which reached levels openly mocked by their Cuban colleagues serving in Angola during the second half of the 1980s: the Cubans severely criticised the Soviets for their inclination to plan what they dubbed 'Berlin-style' operations: large-scale, multi-prong advances of mechanised forces, supported by plentiful artillery, aiming for the enemy's centre of gravity – all of which proved ill-suited to cope with even minor insurgencies in Africa. Nevertheless, such experiences were completely ignored by the GenStab and the Soviet operational art remained the centrepiece of the VSRF's doctrine all the way to 2022. Correspondingly, the SV was equipped, trained, and organised to conduct large-scale offensive operations into the enemy's depth, and sought to achieve victory through:

- A) destroying the enemy's armed forces to the level where these could not be expected to regenerate and continue the struggle; or
- B) destroying their ability to operate as a cohesive system

For these reasons the GenStab designed the SV to operate in the form of several echelons. The first was tasked with assaulting enemy positions along multiple axes, searching for a weak spot: as soon as a breakthrough was achieved, the second echelon was to exploit the breakthrough and drive at best speed deep into the rear. The latter was the very purpose for existence of the sizeable VDV Corps: to have the capability to reach out and seize objectives in the enemy rear, thus making the advance easier for the SV. In similar fashion, Naval Infantry was trained to conduct amphibious landings in the enemy's rear whenever the theatre of operation bordered on the sea. For all the above-listed reasons, virtually all Russian ground units – including the VDV – were, essentially, mechanised. At least as important was the firepower factor: every BTG packed a lot of artillery, Russia's traditional 'God of War'.

At the operational and tactical levels, the SV was thus designed and equipped to manoeuvre by fire: to saturate selected enemy positions with immense volumes of indirect fire deployed over a short period of time, to pave the way for a mechanised blow, followed by rapid exploitation in the form of mobile warfare into the enemy's depth. Even when in defence, the VSRF sought to stop the enemy in similar fashion, counterattack, and rapidly regain the initiative with the aim of conducting mobile forms of offensive warfare. It was for all these reasons that the SV had a large corps of engineers, lavishly equipped with obstacle and water-crossing equipment and pontoon bridges, and that its troops intensively trained bridge-laying operations. The emphasis upon the firepower of artillery reached such proportions that some termed the SV as 'an artillery army with a lot of combat vehicles'.[27]

The emphasis on firepower in combination to mobility was not limited to artillery, yet it came at the price of protection in a number of critical weapons systems. The BMP, BMD and BTR families of vehicles packed significant firepower, but were less well protected than their Western counterparts.

However, as subsequent developments were to reveal, the VSRF was suffering from a number of critical flaws. While having a large number of BTGs in 'ready-to-fight' condition, it possessed no reserves to replace losses, and was experiencing immense problems whenever trying to rebuild worn-out units. This problem was made even more complex by the fact that even its professional soldiers were specialised in only one function and retained that specialisation for their entire career. The BTG system offered high levels of flexibility in the so-called 'hybrid' wars and expeditionary campaigns of the 2010s: however, all were characterised by their relatively short duration, which enabled the VSRF to quickly replace 'spent' units with new BTGs. In turn, the same system was to quickly prove unviable and unbalanced: BTGs wielded tremendous amounts of firepower, and were – if fully equipped – adequately protected against air power, but were always critically short on infantry. For example, even under ideal conditions, a motor rifle platoon mounted in BMP-2s had only 32 soldiers, of which nine were vehicle crew: only 21 were soldiers trained to fight while dismounted. In reality, and because the entire VSRF was short of personnel, many motor rifle platoons sent into Ukraine had only enough personnel to crew their vehicles: they included none, or next to none, of the infantry necessary to protect those vehicles. Such BTGs were to prove hopelessly inadequate for fighting a prolonged conventional war against the conventional armed forces of Ukraine.

This was even more true because it soon turned out that many vehicles deployed by the VSRF were in poor technical condition and thus sensitive to mechanical breakdowns; that the logistics were entirely inadequate for any kind of long-ranged advances along the roads; and that while relatively well-designed and armed, most Russian MBTs, IFVs, and APCs were horrendously vulnerable to any kind of combat damage.[28]

Command-by-Plan

The emphasis on firepower, manoeuvre, and speed entailed a specific way of command – because in the Russian way of war, time was always essential. For this reason, chronically overtasked officers of the SV were trained to operate in a heavily scripted fashion, while applying a set of standardised tactical procedures, custom-developed by the GenStab for every imaginable situation – instead of engaging in the time-consuming process of analysing the situation and then producing tailor-made plans for specific situations on the battlefield. The aim of such thinking and planning was to outpace the enemy's own decision-making process. This also conditioned the logistics system of the SV: it was over-reliant on railways, and in deep trouble whenever it had to support a large segment of the force beyond a point about 25km from the last available railway head. Moreover, it sustained its units through a 'push' system, where the depots would send standard shipments of ammunition, fuel, and supplies on the basis of precalculated average consumption. That said, the Russian logistics system was fundamentally different to that of the West in depending on railway transportation rather than trucks, and at the strategic as well as operational level. The organisation of this system was regularly honed during large-scale annual exercises, during which the VSRF proved capable of moving large numbers of units around the country at short notice. Arguably, 10 truck-equipped logistic brigades were established, but only tasked with hauling supplies from the railway heads over some 20–40km to the frontline at the tactical level. Neither the railway nor the truck logistics ever made use of palettes or standardised crates: every single box of ammunition, food or other supplies had to be reloaded by hand.

At least as problematic was the Russian failure to convert the VKS into a war-winning branch. Arguably, the air force had been re-equipped with big and powerful multi-role combat aircraft – or fighter-bombers – supposedly capable of fighting air-to-air as much as air-to-ground. However, except for the most experienced amongst them, the mass of its crews was never trained for more than one task. The air force was never equipped with a significant quantity of PGMs, nor navigation and attack pods to increase the precision of those that were available. Finally – and contrary to the Soviet military thinking, where the former Frontal Aviation was expected to win an air war by decisive and massive blows against enemy air defences early during the war, so to become free to support friendly ground forces, in the VSRF the purpose of the aviation was severely limited. The counter-air task – strikes on enemy air bases and air defences – was assigned to strategic bombers armed with cruise missiles and to ground-launched tactical ballistic missiles. Although the VKS of 2022 was equipped with airborne early warning aircraft (like the Beriyev A-50) and flying command posts (like the Ilyushin Il-20M), its air defence operations were to be conducted only within the frame of an IADS controlled by ground forces, consisting of a dense array of ground-based air defence systems. That said, the principal task of the aviation was reduced to that of providing support for ground forces on the frontline with free-fall bombs and unguided rockets.

Overall, this 'command-by-the-plan' philosophy was a double-edged sword: it allowed for a fast decision-making process but hindered initiative while generating a lack of flexibility. Russian officers were trained to operate following very specific patterns, while decisions about unforwarded developments were retained by the uppermost level of command. This in turn meant that while the entire system was fast when in possession of the initiative, it was slow whenever in a reactive mode. Similarly, the logistic system was frail, because combat units carried with them only enough food for 2–3 days, fuel for fewer, and no spare parts: they were supposed to be kept supplied by logistic brigades (usually one per combined arms army), which were to prove slow, inflexible, and inadequate in their capacity, while consuming almost all of the technically-versed personnel.

3
PUTIN'S CANNON FODDER

One of the stated goals of the massive military assault on Ukraine in February 2022 was a 'response to a call for aid' from the self-declared Donetsk People's Republic and the Luhansk People's Republic – two para-states existent on the territory of eastern Ukraine for eight years. Rather than directly annexing them, like Crimea, the Kremlin officially recognised them only on 21 February 2022, and then explicitly within their 'pre-2014 oblast boundaries', i.e. as the two oblasts while they had been part of Ukraine – and this even though the DPR and the LPR controlled only around a third of the territory in question.[1]

Armed Formations of the DPR and the LPR
Unlike the seizure of Crimea, conducted by Spetsnaz and VDV troops, the conflict fought in the Donbass region of 2014–2015 was a much more chaotic affair, resulting in the establishment of Separatist armed formations. Emboldened by Moscow, a group of around 50 people led by Igor 'Strelkov' Girkin crossed the border and ignited an armed insurgency by seizing administrative buildings in Slovyansk on 12 April 2014. As the fighting spread, small groups of fighters coalesced, loosely grouped into what became known as the Donbass People's Militia. Uprisings in other major urban centres

A T-64BV captured from the Ukrainian armed forces, seen while being operated by the LPR forces in the spring of 2022. (Russian MOD)

eventually resulted in the declarations of the DPR and the LPR, but a pro-Russian insurgency in Kharkiv was quickly crushed, while the 'massive surge of public support' for the 'People's Republics' expected by Girkin and his followers did not materialise. Indeed, as the ZSU gathered pace over the second half of 2014, the DPR and LPR were forced to withdraw from all the cities they had captured initially, including Severodonetsk and Lysychansk in the Luhansk oblast, and Slovyansk, Kramatorsk, and Mariupol in the Donetsk. Indeed, by August 2014, Ukrainian forces were in the process of encircling Donetsk when the Kremlin chose to launch its own military intervention. This culminated in the battle of Debaltseve in February 2015, a few days after the signing of the Minsk II Agreement, and represented the last major territorial change prior to February 2022.

Build-up of the Armed Formations of the DPR and LPR
After Minsk II, the Kremlin sought to reorganise the Donbass People's Militia. This involved pulling the numerous 'battalions' into a formalised structure under a unified chain of command, and 'removing' – by any means necessary – several violent and unruly commanders. After the initial talk about a 'united Novorossiya', including a unified military command, the leaders of the DPR and the LPR proved unwilling to create a single political and military entity, and instead subordinated their armed formations to the DPR's I Army Corps and the LPR's II Army Corps. Over the following seven years, the Kremlin poured significant resources into their development, although practicing the policy of 'plausible deniability' all the time. For example, it provided numerous older BMP-1 and BMP-2 IFVs, but none of the newer BMP-3s; quite a few older T-64 MBTs and earlier models of T-72s, but none of their modern variants; finally, it provided vast numbers of Ural 43206 4x4 military utility trucks, but no GAZ Tigr light utility vehicles, because the latter were ubiquitous in the VSRF.

That said, there remained uncertainty about the level of integration of the DPR and LPR's armed formations, with some analysts assessing that the I and II Army Corps were formal extensions of the 8th Combined Arms Army, Southern OSK, VSRF, although the unruly and often chaotic nature of these formations suggested something else, while captured DPR troops later reported some units – like the 100th Motor Rifle Brigade 'Republican Guards' – not only receiving T-72Bs from Russia, but also having Russian

The level of integration of DPR and LPR armed forces was always a topic of much controversy. It is only in recent years that additional details are becoming known. This photograph shows Major Vitaly Sukuev (right), VDV officer who commanded the 1st 'Khan' Spetsnaz Battalion in early 2015. Sukuev was killed in Ukraine while commanding the 108th VDV Regiment in September 2022. (RSOTM)

commanders.[2] That said, powerful local commanders were able to act almost autonomously, and coordination was frequently lacking, while top commanders and politicians were usually removed by 'political' or other means. For example, in 2017, the leader of the LPR, Igor Plotnitsky, was removed in a coup which placed Leonid Pasechnik in control. A year later, Alexander Zakharchenko, the leader of the DPR, was assassinated in a bomb blast in central Donetsk, and replaced by Denish Pushilin – a Separatist leader generally seen as 'more willing to cooperate with the Kremlin'.

Eventually, by early 2022, the I Army Corps controlled five brigades (four motorised rifle and one artillery), and two motorised rifle regiments, as well as several independent battalions, with a total strength of about 20,000. The LPR's II Army Corps had a strength of four brigades (three motorised rifle and one artillery), one motorised rifle regiment and a number of battalions, with about 15,000 combatants. These units were arrayed along the 250-kilometre-long 'Line of Control' (LOC) facing ZSU units, with each of the DPR and LPR motorised rifle brigades controlling its own sector. An unusual anomaly was the 2nd Motor Rifle Brigade of the LPR, which controlled the towns of Debaltseve and Horlivka in the DPR.

About 80 kilometres of the LOC was delineated by the Siversky Donets River: this included the crucial sectors of Stanytsia Luhanska and Shchastia. Most of the bridges across the river were destroyed, a key exception being the road bridge at the latter town, where the ZSU retained a heavily fortified bridgehead on the southern bank.

4
LAST-MINUTE MOVES

With hindsight, it appears easy to conclude that Putin's planning for the (re-)invasion of Ukraine in 2022, was based on little more than irrational illusions, and thus flawed from the beginning. However, when studying his way of rule and his decision-making, one should keep in mind a number of crucial experiences of the strongman in Moscow, and the way he perceived the world around him. He saw the West, quite cynically, leaving Russia to its own devices as long as it watched its nuclear weapons, supplied the West with oil and gas, and squandered billions on luxury goods: nobody minded when Putin, driven by corrupt Soviet imperialism, revanchism, and hatred and jealousy over the Ukrainian decision to choose Europe embarked on a mission of controlling Ukraine, and nobody minded his fear

of both the Ukrainian and Western parliamentary democracies. In turn, his experience from provoking wars in Chechnya, in Georgia, from the military interventions in Syria and elsewhere was that a quick war supported by immense volumes of propaganda was a solution to all of his problems – because it raised his approval ratings, while mobilising Russian society and distracting it from growing internal problems. Correspondingly, from Putin's point of view, a new invasion and complete defeat of Ukraine was a simple yet most promising option.

Military Build-Up

Putin's planning for an all-out invasion of Ukraine probably began as early as of 2015–2017; at least it was in that period that a series of 'accidents' destroyed the largest depots of artillery ammunition in Ukraine. Amongst these were depots in Svatove (containing 3,500 tons of ammunition, which blew up on 29 October 2016), Balakliya (the second largest ammunition depot of the ZSU, which blew up on 23 March 2017, and again on 3 May 2018 and 15 November 2019), Kalynivka (a depot containing 32,000 tons of ammunition, on 26 September 2017), and Ichnia (9 October 2018). The losses de-facto destroyed the ZSU's strategic stocks of artillery ammunition: the extent of the damage caused becomes clear when considering that according to reports in the Ukrainian press, the ZSU expended a total of 24,000 tons of ammunition during the fighting of 2014–2015. Of course, the Kremlin denied any kind of involvement in any of these events, while the West characterised the affairs in question as, essentially, accidents, caused by the lack of care for stores of old, Soviet-era ammunition.[3]

Certainly enough, it took Putin years to set the scene: negotiations for new gas-pipelines, contracts for gas- and oil-exports until 2040, the subversion of multiple EU and NATO governments, and that of the USA – all proved time consuming affairs costing the strongman in Kremlin a lot of his 'black cash', but: in turn they secured the financing of the further military build-up and, ultimately, the new adventure in Ukraine. Moreover, such measures on the international scene were supported by gradually escalating propaganda warfare at home, which eventually convinced the Russian public that Ukraine was ruled by a NATO-installed Nazi regime, and preparing an invasion of not only the self-declared DPR and LPR, but a genocide of their populations, followed by an invasion of Russia.

Eventually, it was only in 2021, when the USA and allies decided to withdraw from Afghanistan, that Putin felt his moment had come. In March that year, the VSRF began deploying units along the border of Ukraine. The process was intensified in April, and especially in September of the same year, all under the guise of preparing another of the *Zapad* (West) major military exercises, conducted frequently during earlier years. Although the US and British intelligence services began issuing alerts in November 2021, their reporting was compromised by the fact that over the last 30 years similar assessments regarding Iraq and Afghanistan were either flatly wrong, or intentionally misinforming, or massively misused by the political leadership in Washington and London. Indeed, in most of the European part of the NATO – and thus in Ukraine, too – the seriousness of the situation became obvious only in January 2022, when the entire 35th CAA from the Far East MD and the 41st CAA from the Central MD were redeployed to Belarus. Even then, the predominant opinion was that 'Putin isn't going to do it'. In February 2022, the entire 1st Guards Tank Army – widely considered to be the VSRF's best equipped and trained troops, and usually held back as an operational reserve – was redeployed from its garrisons in the Moscow area to the border of Ukraine. These moves dramatically expanded the potential length of the front lines that the Ukrainians would have to defend in the case of an attack. Overall, by the middle of that month, the VSRF had a staggering 127 BTGs arrayed around the border, in addition to nine motor rifle brigades, two motor rifle regiments, and two artillery brigades of the LPR and the DPR. This was an unprecedented concentration of conventional armed forces in Europe since 1945.

How this 'armada' was meant to fight an all-out, conventional war with Ukraine remains unclear. Partially based on captured Russian military documentation, the information available as of the summer of 2022 was that the FSB assessed the cultural and historic links between Russia and Ukraine as being so close that the majority of Ukrainian soldiers would rather lay down their arms and join the VSRF than oppose an invasion. Such impressions were only bolstered by Western intelligence assessments, many of which not only had the doubts about the Ukrainian will to resist, but about the very capability of the ZSU to mount anything more than token resistance – of which the FSB and the GRU seems to have been aware. Correspondingly, Putin, Shoygu, and Gerasimov devised a plan that was an enlarged repeat of the exercise from Crimea of 2014, and at least broadly similar to Operation Danube, the Soviet-led intervention of the Warsaw Pact forces in Czechoslovakia of 1968. At the same time, they were so certain of success, that they never went to the trouble of actually informing the VSRF about its task.[4]

Special Military Operation

According to the final version of the plan for what Putin and his supporters termed the 'Special Military Operation', the Russian special forces, PMCs, and Airborne Assault Troops were to quickly secure at least one or two of the five major airports outside Kyiv, then receive reinforcements and assault into the so-called 'Triangle' – the governmental district in the downtown – to arrest or kill President Volodimir Zelensky and members of his cabinet, thus paralysing the government, and then organise a handover to a Moscow-friendly regime. Meanwhile, conventional units of the VSRF were to cross the border and then dash for Kyiv from the north and north-east, securing Chernihiv, Sumy, Kharkiv and Poltava. However, of even more importance was the plot for the conquest of eastern and southern Ukraine, where the VSRF was expected to secure all of the Luhansk, Donetsk, Zaproizhzhya, Kherson, and Odesa oblasts – which were then to be annexed to Russia – and to establish a land connection to the Russian separatists in Transnistria. Above all, this was never meant to be a 'war' – but a 'special military operation': an enterprise expected to be conducted in the form of a quick coup, accompanied by decapitating strikes and high-speed power demonstrations, aimed at instilling fear and respect into any enemies and opposition, at home and abroad, and officially carried out with the intention of de-nazifying and demilitarising Ukraine within 10–14 days. The original D-Day was set for 20 February 2022.

While this might appear as another high-risk gamble by Putin, for the reasons described above it did not appear as such *to him*. A combination of endemic corruption and incompetence resulted in severe misreporting, which resulted in a dismissive stance towards Ukrainians and an entirely unrealistic assessment of the VSRF's capabilities. Convinced of his own skills as a grand strategist and military genius, and succumbing to illusions about the mass of Ukrainians being unwilling to resist – indeed, willing to join their brotherly Russians, bolstered by the FSB's 'best case' reporting, partially based on similar Western military intelligence assessments – Putin ignored the VSRF's chain of command before the first shot was fired, while not having even a remote grip on the situation. In the same way that he ruled the Russian Federation without a political program, but through TV shows and decrees, during the build-up to invasion, he further worsened the situation through redeploying and redistributing military units away from their commands, from one tactical army to another, thus creating constantly growing problems with their coordination and logistics. Driven by the requirement to score propaganda points at home, he began assigning tasks to selected, favourite commanders, without consideration for the VSRF's doctrine: indeed, the latter was literally 'thrown out of the

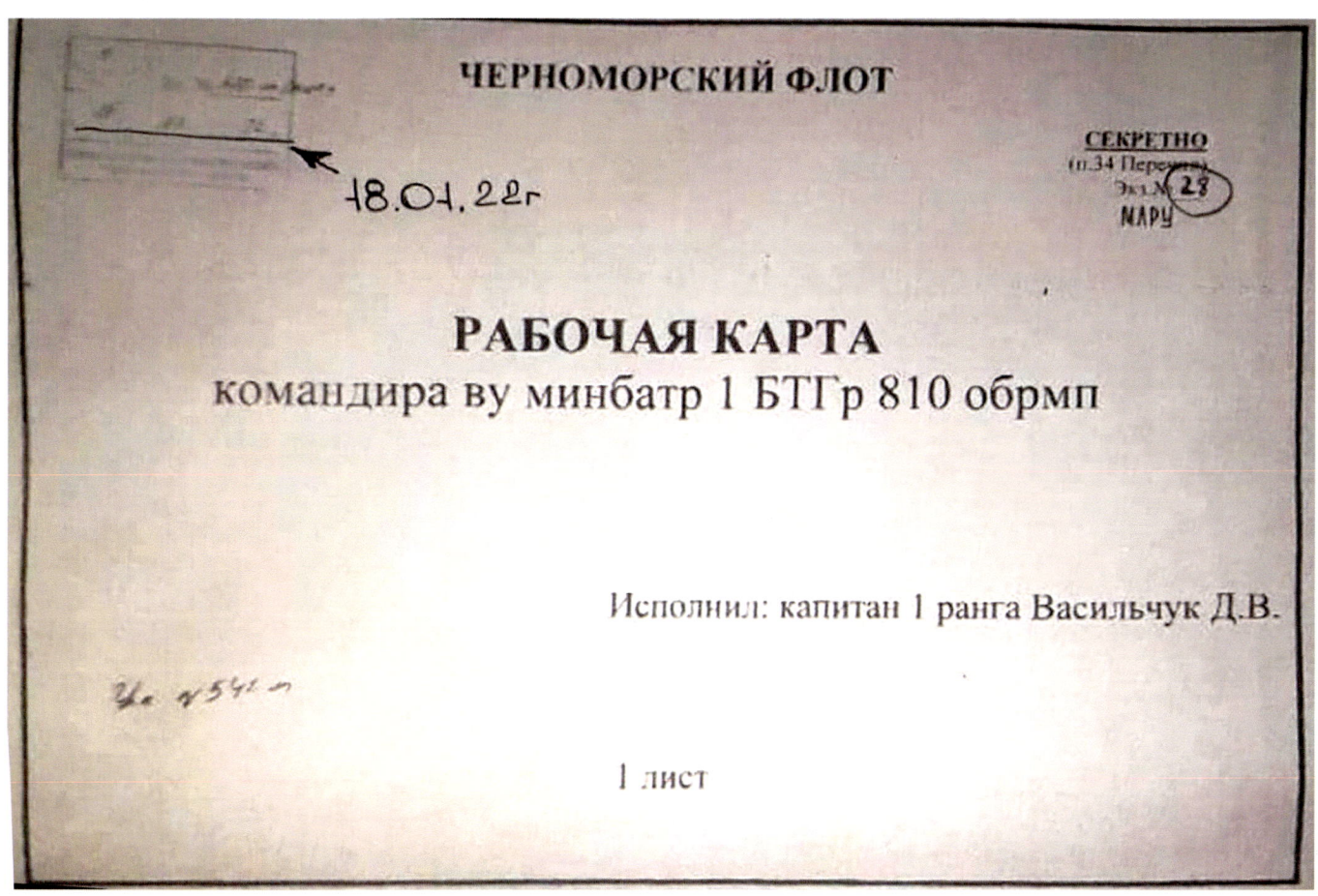

The front page of the plan for the invasion of Ukraine as issued by the HQ of the 810th Naval Infantry Brigade (58th CAA). (Ukrainian MOD)

A page from the same document, showing the planned start of the operation against Ukraine as 20 February and its end as 6 March 2022. (Ukrainian MOD) window', resulting in a situation where the headquarters of two military districts responsible for the pending operation – OSK West and OSK South – were assigned the command of units (and thus the responsibility of keeping them supplied) that they did not effectively control; where lightly armed airborne units were sent into assaults on heavily protected installations without the support of their heavy weapons; where mechanised units trained to operate in open plains of western Russia were ordered to secure densely built-up urban areas, and where the Air Force was merely deployed to strike selected points with cruise missiles, and then fly VDV troops to their targets. The logistic chain of the VSRF was already overstrained before the invasion began; equipment was moved to mustering points, followed by troops; however, they all carried too few supply reserves with them to reach their objectives, and the few organic refuelling trucks were far from enough to make do. In other words: through all of the corruption, incompetence and ineptitude of its commanders, the VSRF did not really fail in Ukraine: it was doomed to fail due to the 'System Putin', and on order from Putin.

This became clear by May 2022, when the Western intelligence services obtained enough evidence about the strongman's involvement in the planning and conduct of VSRF operations down to the level of battalion tactical groups, to reveal this to the media. Correspondingly, and right from the start, Putin was micromanaging the entire campaign in Ukraine through bypassing the established chain of command and issuing orders directly to commanders of BTGs, sometimes even below that level.[5]

Consequences

During the build-up to the invasion, the VSRF deployed nine armies around Ukraine, arrayed clockwise as follows:

- 35th CAA, deployed in southern Belarus, including over a dozen of its own BTGs and elements of the 29th and 36th CAAs, several VDV units, the 31st VDV and the 45th Spetsnaz Brigade reinforced by Redut PMC, Rosgvardia and SOBR elements, all tasked with securing Kyiv.
- 41st CAA, deployed in south-eastern Belarus, including at least 10 BTGs, and tasked with securing Chernihiv before continuing for Kyiv.
- 2nd Guards Combined Arms Army (GCAA), with at least nine BTGs, tasked with securing Konotop, followed by an advance on Kyiv from the east.
- 1st Guards Tank Army (GTA), including about 24 BTGs – mostly from its own formations, but including two BTGs from the 200th 'Arctic' Motor Rifle Brigade – tasked with the seizure of Sumy and Poltava.
- 6th CAA, reinforced to a total of about 11 BTGs through units from the 1st GTA and the 20th CAA, tasked with securing Kharkiv in cooperation with the 20th CAA.
- 20th CAA, including five BTGs of the VSRF and at least three BTGs of Redut PMC, and also controlling all the units of the II Army Corps LPR, tasked with securing the Luhansk Oblast and then outflanking the LOC from the north.
- 8th CAA, including its eight BTGs and the units of the I Army Corps DPR, tasked with securing Mariupol and then outflanking the LOC from the south.
- 58th CAA, including 14 BTGs, tasked with securing Zaporizhzhya Oblast, helping take Mariupol and thus establishing a land corridor between the DPR and the Crimea.
- 49th CAA, including 15 BTGs, tasked with rapid advance on Kherson, Mykolaiv, Odessa, and establishment of a land corridor to Transnistria.[6]

Ukraine's Reluctant Build-up

Despite the sad state of the Ukrainian Navy, and unsatisfactory condition of the Air Force, in grand total the ZSU had managed to evolve into a potent force by 2022 – definitely a far cry from what it had been in 2014. Once a defeated institution, the Ukrainians engaged in a period of fierce self-criticism and fast-paced reforms, similar to those of the Egyptian armed forces between 1967 and 1973. As a result, the primary strength of the ZSU lay in its combat-hardened ground forces, meanwhile retrained to operate in a far more flexible way through improved training – and empowerment – of junior officers and NCOs.

The primary problem was that the mass of regular ZSU units was deployed along the LOC in the Donbass, while the mass of units based elsewhere around the country was either not mobilised, or mobilised too late to take part in the first few weeks of the Russian invasion.

Another problem remained the combination of insufficient funding and widespread corruption within the officer corps – two phenomena that plagued the country as a whole: in this regard, reforms instigated after 2014 never went as far as intended. That said, the issue of corruption was exaggerated by NATO advisors dissatisfied whenever Ukrainians refused to follow their advice. In this regards it should be kept in mind that after spending 50 years preparing to fight a major war against the USSR and Warsaw Pact, for the last 30 years the armed forces of the transatlantic alliance were busy fighting relatively minor armed conflicts with an emphasis on counterinsurgency operations and while enjoying absolute aerial superiority. On the contrary, the stubborn and independently-minded Ukrainians rapidly accumulated immense volumes of combat experience in conventional warfare against a 'peer' opponent – which was something their NATO allies completely lacked. Ukrainians could not afford to reform and bolster all the branches of the ZSU at the same time and to a similar degree: for them, it was crucial to reinforce the ground forces because these were necessary to continue guarding the LOC and most promising in regards of possible defence from a renewed Russian aggression. Therefore, the Air Force and Navy – traditionally high-technology branches and a priority in the West – clearly lagged behind in their development, resulting in underestimation of actual Ukrainian combat capacities by Western military experts.

Finally, due to modern-day Ukraine having a rich history of turncoats and traitors, the perhaps biggest issue many Western advisors deployed in the country since 2014 had, was uncertainty if the armed forces would actually fight a renewed Russian aggression, or fold up and fall apart, or even defect en masse and join the aggressors. With hindsight, and combined with corruption and at least some incompetence within the officer corps, this was an issue that heavily influenced many foreign observers in Ukraine to underestimate the ZSU; indeed, to conclude it would offer little more than feeble resistance before being overrun – in a matter of between three days and two weeks. Perhaps less vocally, a very few – correctly – assessed that the Ukrainians had come a long way not only in regards of their national conscience, but to become a force to be reckoned with. Amongst the latter was Major General David S Baldwin, of the California Air National Guard, who – after being intensively committed to supporting the Ukrainian training efforts – observed:

Because we work closely with the Ukrainian army, we always thought that the West underestimated them, and the National Guard of Ukraine also. We knew that they had radically improved their ability to do kind of Western-style military decision making. I have been impressed though, with their ability at the national level, to work through some of the challenges we thought they still had in terms of logistics and command control. I think the best story is with their Air Force. Our fighter pilots have been telling everyone for years that the Ukrainian Air Force is pretty good. And in the meantime, a lot of other people in the West were pooh-poohing them.[7]

Welcome to Hell

While the mass of details about Putin's activity in relation to the invasion of Ukraine, and the VSRF's build-up and preparations for this can be made out with the help of a thorough cross-examination of reports in the mainstream and social media, much less is known about the final Ukrainian preparations. Part of the reason is that many of the initial activities of the ZSU in reaction to the unprovoked aggression remain shrouded in mystery, weather because of understandable concerns for operational security, an equally understandable chaos at the start of any armed conflict, plain and unavoidable failures, military incompetence and outright treachery, or because of casualties amongst participants since. That said, the strategic situation of the Ukrainian armed forces can be assessed with a reasonable degree of certainty.

According to unofficial Ukrainian sources, Zelensky finally realised that an invasion was imminent and ordered a mobilisation of at least the Reserve 1 – thus enabling active brigades to be fully staffed – on Friday 18 February. Simultaneously, and although the political leadership of Ukraine remained insistent that there would be no war (primarily because European officials were all the time assuring that 'Putin would not do that', but also because their military intelligence services concluded that the VSRF lacked the force to conquer a city the size of Kyiv), the ZSU redeployed all of its major headquarters to alternative positions: away from the probable targets of the opening Russian strike. This decision was considered sensitive enough for Kyiv not to inform any of its Western allies about it. Three days later, the Commander-in-Chief ZSU, Gencral Valerii Fedorovych Zaluzhnyi, forwarded the following message to the VSRF in Russian, using social media: 'You will attack us at 10:1 and 15:1 ratios. We will not meet you with flowers. We will meet you with guns. Welcome to Hell!'

Correspondingly, during the last few days before the attack, Ukrainian troops sprayed 'Welcome to hell!' on many of the overpasses and traffic signs along highways close to the Russian border. More importantly, by the evening of 23 February, the bulk of the regular ZSU was in the process of mobilisation and dispersal, a few units even in their waiting positions deeper inside Ukraine, a few in defence positions on the approach to major urban centres, while units deployed along the LOC remained in their positions.[8]

5
THE FIRST WEEK OF THE THREE-DAY INVASION[1]

During the afternoon and evening of 23 February, under pretence of preparing for yet another major exercise, the VSRF units arrayed around Ukraine moved into jump-off positions along the border. Putin's fateful aggression was now just a matter of time.

Opening Blows

At 04.15hrs in the morning of 24 February 2022, Kyiv time, in a TV announcement pre-recorded on the evening of 21 February, Putin declared war on Ukraine. The aggression began at 05.00hrs with severe jamming of all frequency bands and the harassment of Ukrainian early warning radars by E95M decoy UAVs simulating Russian aircraft.[2] The Russians also launched a major cyber-attack on the websites of the Ukrainian government, another aiming to disrupt the high-voltage electrical sub-stations in Ukraine, and an attempt to disrupt the US satellite communications provider Viasat's operations in the country. As a consequence, they managed to temporarily knock out the strategic communication system of the ZSU: to interrupt links between the GenStab-U, the Operational Commands, and all the brigades.[3]

There followed several waves of ballistic and cruise missiles, mostly targeting Ukrainian air bases and airports, but relatively

Opening Russian ballistic and cruise missile barrage included the deployment of dozens of Iskander-M tactical ballistic missiles which targeted key command nodes and troop concentrations of the ZSU. This photograph was taken during an exercise in 2018. (Russian MOD)

few air defence bases. Ukrainian air defences were not on alert, and thus over 60 percent of Russian cruise missiles reached their target entirely undisturbed. However, exactly as over Syria in 2015–2016, a significant number malfunctioned, often leaving bedazzled Ukrainians to wonder why the Russians were wasting missiles with a price tag of US$1 million to target empty fields. There were exceptions, too: one of the most heavily hit locations was the base of the 164th Radar Brigade, outside Kharkiv, which was savaged by multiple Iskander strikes: the unit lost several radars and transporter-erector-launchers (TELs) for its S-300s.

The tactical aviation of the VKS flew relatively few strikes by design: its primary tasks were to strike selected Ukrainian command posts along the LOC and support the onslaught on Kyiv. The MOD in Moscow claimed the involvement of 75 aircraft: amongst them strategic bombers that released cruise missiles, and Su-34 and Su-35S fighter-bombers armed with Kh-58 anti-radar missiles (ASCC/NATO-codename 'AS-11 Kilter'), that targeted radars of those Ukrainian air defence units that had powered up in reaction to the missile strikes, and were close enough to the border. Generally, due to the last-minute evacuation of the Ukrainian Air Force's aircraft from bases in the north and east of the country in a south-western direction, the Russians caught next to no enemy aircraft on the ground. One exception was a Su-27 confirmed as destroyed on the tarmac of Ozerne AB in the Zhitomir area. Instead, the Russians encountered several Ukrainian interceptors in the air, and are known to have shot down the Su-27 piloted by Major Dmitry Kolomiets, who was killed.[4]

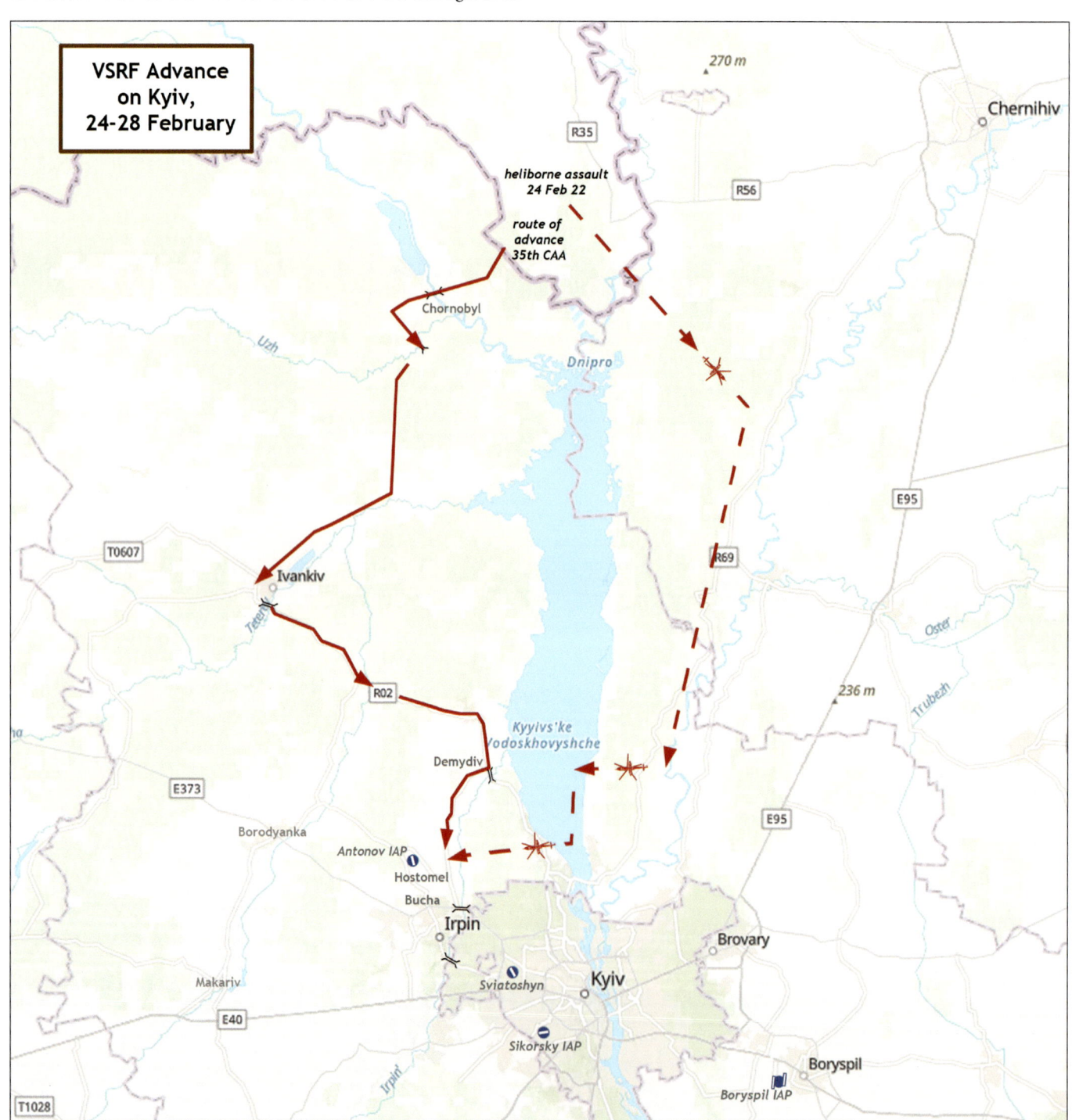

A map of the 35th CAA's principal route of advance on Kyiv, 24–28 February 2022, and the heliborne assault on Hostomel, on the first morning of the war. (Map by Tom Cooper)

The 9K720 Iskander-M (ASCC/NATO-codename 'SS-26 Stone') is a mobile, short-range ballistic missile, in service with the VSRF since 2006. Its primary purpose is to strike enemy air defences, command posts, and communication nodes, or troop concentrations out to a range of 500km. The 4,615kg 9M723K1 is a single-stage solid-propellant missile, which can be retargeted during flight, and has an optically guided warhead with self-homing capability. It flies at hypersonic speeds (Mach 6–7) and had an advertised Circular Error Probable of 5–7 metres with the optical homing head, or 30–70m in autonomous operation. Iskander-Ms deployed against Ukraine reportedly employed decoys to confuse ZSU air defence systems. (Artwork by David Bocquelet)

Developed in the 1980s, the 2S19/2S19M Msta-S self-propelled 152mm howitzer was the most advanced and most widely used weapons system of this type in service with both the VSRF and the ZSU as of February 2022. Weighing 42 tonnes, it is capable of firing 6–8 rounds per minute over a range of 24.7km, and with base bleed shells over 29–36km. Between 400 and 500 such systems were available to Russian formations for the invasion of Ukraine: most of them served with two 'divisions' in each artillery brigade. Combined with Orlan-10 UAVs, they proved highly effective. This artwork is based on a VSRF-operated example photographed in north-eastern Ukraine early during the war. (Artwork by David Bocquelet)

Entering service in the early 1970s, the 2S1 Gvozdika was the first modern self-propelled howitzer of Soviet design. Based on the MT-LBu multipurpose chassis, it mounted the 2A18 122mm howitzer with a range of 15.3km using conventional shells. Ukraine inherited 638 from the USSR, and this fleet was reinforced by 49 examples acquired from the Czech Republic. These vehicles formed the backbone of the ZSU's artillery brigades, and of its artillery groups assigned to tank and mechanised brigades. The hull has also been used as a base for the Kevlar-E IFV. This relatively rare example serving with the Russian VSRF was sighted in northern Ukraine in late February 2022. (Artwork by David Bocquelet)

Airborne Assault units (VDV) of the Russian Armed Forces formed the spearhead of most operations in the first days of the invasion of February 2022. Like the rest of the VSRF, they were completely mechanised, and equipped with custom-designed light armoured vehicles. The most advanced of these was the BMD-4 IFV, weighing 13.6 tons, and armed with the 2A70 low-pressure 100mm rifled gun, the 2A72 coaxial 30mm cannon, and a 7.62mm PKT machine gun. The BMD-4 has a crew of three and can carry up to five passengers. This example served with a VDV unit assigned to the 35th CAA. (Artwork by David Bocquelet)

Still the most numerous armoured fighting vehicle of the VDV as of 2022, was the BMD-2. Dating back to the mid-1980s, it is armed with the 2A42 30mm autocannon, and a 7.62mm PKT coaxial machine gun. Many BMD-2s deployed in Ukraine in 2022 were also equipped with the pintle-mounted the 9P135M-1 ATGM launcher, shown above the turret. The BMD-2 has a crew of two and can carry six dismounts. This example was sighted in the Kherson area in early March 2022. (Artwork by David Bocquelet)

This BMD-2 of the 31st Airborne Assault Brigade is shown as it appeared in the Hostomel area on 24–26 February. The vehicle was left painted in its dark green overall colour, and had a number of metal or wooden planks added to the sides of the hull to bolster protection. The BMD-2's armour of welded aluminium alloy – 15mm thick at the front and lower hull, but only 7mm on the sides – proved highly vulnerable even to machine gun fire and attrition was heavy. (Artwork by David Bocquelet)

WAR IN UKRAINE VOLUME 2: RUSSIAN INVASION, FEBRUARY 2022

Introduced to service back in 1974, the BTR-D was the armoured personnel carrier counterpart of the BMD and used to supplement the latter in specialist roles in the VDV. Instead of a turret, it had two bow-mounted PKT machine guns, sometimes replaced by PKBs (shown here) or AGS-17 grenade launchers. As of 2022, they still served with the 7th, 76th, 98th, and 106th Guards Airborne Assault Divisions, but were frequently used as weapons carriers, or command vehicles. This example was sighted in the Hostomel area, and probably assigned to the 31st Airborne Assault Brigade. (Artwork by David Bocquelet)

The BTR-MDM came into being as a further development of the BMD-3 armoured fighting vehicles of the VDV. It has a significantly bigger superstructure instead of a turret, and is suitable for use as a command vehicle, troop transport, and to haul fuel, ammunition, or evacuate wounded personnel. Proving highly popular in service, many were added to formations in addition to their nominal strength. This example, armed with an AGS-17 automatic grenade launcher – in addition to the RPK machine gun – was seen in the Hostomel area in late February 2022. (Artwork by David Bocquelet)

The BTR-82A is the latest production version of the BTR-82 armoured personnel carrier, with a more powerful engine, improved armour, spall liners, and night vision devices. The main visible difference compared to the earlier variant is the installation of the 2A72 30mm autocanon. Most BTGs of the VSRF motor rifle and Naval Infantry regiments included a company equipped with 10 of these large vehicles; while some also had additional examples assigned to reconnaissance platoons. This example was sighted in north-eastern Ukraine in late February 2022. (Artwork by David Bocquelet)

Designed as successor to the prolific family of BMP-1 and BMP-2 IFVs, the BMP-3 entered service in the late 1980s: about 2,000 have been manufactured since, but most of those in service with motor rifle formations of the VSRF as of February 2022, were acquired after a major contract for their production was issued by the Russian Ministry of Defence in May 2015. This 18.7-ton vehicle has lightweight armour of aluminium alloys and steel, 35mm thick on the front, but elsewhere offering protection from small arms fire only. Armament consists of a turret-mounted 2K23 100mm gun, with an 2A72 coaxial 30mm autocannon. In addition to a crew of three, it can carry seven troops. This example was knocked out in north-eastern Ukraine early during the invasion of February 2022. (Artwork by David Bocquelet)

Introduced to service in 1980, the BMP-2 is probably the most widely used infantry fighting vehicle in service with the VSRF of recent decades. This 14.3-ton vehicle was a development of the earlier BMP-1, including a turret-mounted 2A42 30mm autocannon. It has a crew of three and can carry up to seven troops. As of February 2022, each of the motor rifle BTGs of the VSRF was supposed to include two companies of 10 BMP-2 or BMP-3 IFVs. Shown here is a BMP-2 as seen in the Antonovsky Bridge area early on 25 February 2022. (Artwork by David Bocquelet)

Ukraine inherited over 1,460 BMP-2s from the former USSR: after many foreign sales and the losses of 2014–2015, around 890 were still in service with its mechanised formations as of 2019. A number of Ukrainian BMP-2s were captured by the Separatists, and then reinforced by some from surplus stocks of the VSRF, enabling units like the 6th Separate Cossacks Motorised Rifle Regiment (LPR) and the 11th Separate Enakievo-Danube Motor Rifle Regiment 'Vostok' (DPR) to establish entire battalions equipped with them. This example, seen in Donetsk in early March 2022, probably belonged to the latter. (Artwork by David Bocquelet)

The MT-LB is a multipurpose, fully amphibious tracked armoured fighting vehicle, manufactured in large numbers since the 1970s, derived from the earlier MT-L over-snow tractor. Initially meant to serve as an armoured artillery tractor, it has a crew of two but can also serve as an APC with the capability to carry 11 passengers. Over 3,300 were still in active service with the VSRF as of February 2022, up to 100 with the armed forces of the DPR and LPR, and up to 2,100 with the ZSU. Many served as weapons carriers: the most frequent was the addition of the ZU-23-2 twin 23mm autocannon atop the superstructure, but the Ukrainians also converted several into the MT-LB-12 version, which had the MT-12 Rapira 100mm anti-tank gun mounted on top of the hull. The example shown here was seen serving with a VSRF unit deployed in north-eastern Ukraine in late February 2022. (Artwork by David Bocquelet)

Developed and manufactured in Kharkiv in the early 1960s and for the rest of that decade, the T-64 was the first tank to use an autoloader for its 125mm smoothbore gun, allowing the reduction of the crew to three, which in turn enabled the vehicle to be of reduced size and weight compared to its Western counterparts. Over 2,000 were inherited by Ukraine from the USSR, and about 20 were captured by the Separatists: this example ended its days serving with the 1st Independent Tank Battalion 'Somalia', of the DPR. It was fitted with a much greater than usual amount of Kontakt-1 ERA along the full length of its side skirts and enlarged turret bustle, and wore a disruptive camouflage pattern in black, dark brown and light green, and a total of 12 red stars, apparently as 'kill markings', on its barrel. (Artwork by David Bocquelet)

The T-72B3M obr. 2016 is one of several upgrades of the T-72B3. It entered production in 2016, and has the same gun, ammunition (including the Svinets-1 and -2 APFSDS rounds with tungsten and depleted uranium penetrators, respectively), the 9K119M Reflex-M system (for the 9M119M Invar ATGMs fired through the gun barrel), and the new generation Relikt ERA-blocks as the T-90M. Its automotive performance was slightly improved through the installation of the more powerful V-92S2F engine and an automatic transmission. Shortly before the invasion of Ukraine, many received 'cage' armour atop their turrets, in an attempt to improve their protection from top-attack weapons like the US-made FGM-148 Javelin. This proved mostly futile, because endemic corruption in Putin's Russia resulted in installation of armour that was of poor quality and Javelins regularly penetrated the cages, or the vehicles were attacked with other types of weaponry. This example belonged either to the 126th Coastal Defence Brigade, or the 20th Motor Rifle Division, and was knocked out in the Voznesensk area, on 2 March 2022. (Artwork by David Bocquelet)

The OTR-21 Tochka (ASCC/NATO-codename 'SS-21 Scarab') is a tactical ballistic missile complex developed in the USSR in the late 1970s, designed to deliver precision strikes on tactical targets such as command posts, bridges, storage depots, troop concentrations, and air bases. Carried by – and fired from – the BAZ-5921 mobile transporter-erector-launcher, its 9M79K missiles can deliver a high-explosive fragmentation warhead over a range of 120km. As of February 2022, the VSRF still had around 200 missiles of this type in service, but they were largely replaced by the much more advanced Iskanders. The ZSU still had up to 90 launchers and about 500 9M79K missiles, and they represented its primary means of striking back at Russian air bases early during the war. (Artwork by David Bocquelet)

The BTR-4 Butsefal is a wheeled infantry fighting vehicle developed as a private venture by the Kharkiv Morozov Machine Building Design Bureau in the mid-2000s. Series production was initiated in 2009, and over 200 were in service with ZSU as of early 2021. Despite apparent problems with export versions, the type proved highly popular in combat operations in 2014, especially because of its good armour and 30mm autocannon. The crews of several examples distinguished themselves in combat against the VSRF during 2022, often taking-on not only on Russian IFVs, but even MBTs. This example was abandoned by the 2nd Battalion, 92nd Mechanised Brigade during its retreat from the Staryi Saltiv area, on 25–26 February 2022. The vehicle was painted in dark green overall, with sand and dark brown applied in the form of 'digital camouflage'. (Artwork by David Bocquelet)

While the Russians rapidly withdrew their T-64s from active service, though later handing over about 50 to the Separatists, the Ukrainians found them better situated to local conditions. They were considered more reliable and, at only 38 tons, lighter than the T-72 series used by the VSRF while offering similar levels of protection. Moreover, the Ukrainians applied numerous modifications to their T-64Bs, the most advanced of which was the T-64BM Bulat (the turret of which is shown inset). Due to the lack of funding, these modifications could not be applied to all the available examples and many went into the battles of 2022 still in their original configuration, wearing the so-called 'digital' camouflage, as illustrated here. (Artwork by David Bocquelet)

Named Gelateika, in honour of the former Minister of Defence, Valery Gelety, the standard uniform of the ZSU was adopted in early 2014, and introduced to service by 2017. It is characterised by the MM14 pixel camouflage, helping to conceal troops in all types of Ukrainian landscape. This sniper is shown wearing the TOR-D helmet (usually issued to special forces), the summer trumpet scarf made of knitted fabric, and the Gelateika's summer field suit, with field jacket that has two chest pockets and two sleeve pockets kept closed by textile fasteners. His weapon is the Zbroyar Z-008 bolt-action 7.62x51mm sniper rifle. (Artwork by Giorgio Albertini)

A large number of volunteers quickly joined the ranks of the ZSU at the start of the war, frequently adding personal gear and armament to the Gelateika uniform. This special forces operator is shown as seen north-west of Kyiv in early March 2022, wearing privately purchased jacket and boots in combination with trousers from the Gelateika uniform. He is shown armed with an assault rifle from the AKM-family, and carrying an FGM-148 Javelin anti-tank guided missile. (Artwork by Giorgio Albertini)

This operator of the 22nd Spetsnaz Brigade, VSRF, is shown as frequently appearing in northern Ukraine in February–March 2022: wearing the Sfera bullet-resistant combat helmet of titanium and steel and the winter version of the Guerrilla Panacea EMR uniform. Atop his jacket he wears the Nazgul tactical vest (with ammunition pouches) and plate carrier. His firearm was the AK-102 – a shortened carabine version of the AK-101 assault rifle, derived from the original AK-47 design, equipped with a telescopic sight and a silencer. (Artwork by Giorgio Albertini)

This soldier of the 31st Airborne Brigade of the VDV is shown as appearing during the assault on Antonov IAP, wearing the shallow helmet of the airborne forces (with cover), and the Spetsnaz Suit 6sh122, with digital Flora pattern. His other gear includes the Spetsnaz tactical vest with ammunition pouches for AKs (worn atop of the plate carrier), a Cascade or Vector backpack, Cross knee pads, and Kobra or Mongoose black leather boots. His firearm is the AK-102 assault rifle. (Artwork by Giorgio Albertini)

Operated by one squadron of the 121st Heavy Bomber Aviation Regiment from Engels Air Base, and by the 182nd Heavy Bomber Aviation Regiment from Ukrainka AB in the Far East, Tupolev Tu-95MS bombers of the VKS were amongst the aircraft to fire the first shots of Putin's all-out attack on 24 February 2022. Only about 50 percent of some 60 airframes still available as of 2022 were fully mission capable at the time. Some had been upgraded to the Tu-95MSM standard, which included new avionics and compatibility with the Kh-555 cruise missile, in addition to earlier Kh-101/Kh-102 and Kh-55 missiles. About a dozen Tu-95MS bombers carried the names of major Russian cities, with this example named after Saratov. (Artwork by Tom Cooper)

A crucial linchpin in operations by the VKS during the attack on Ukraine in February 2022 were Beriev A-50 airborne early warning and control aircraft. Their E-821 Shmel mission system included an S-band radar installed atop a pedestal over the rear fuselage. The radar's search range was around 230km for fighter-size targets at low altitude, or up to 350km at high altitude, and the system could simultaneously track up to 45 targets and 12 friendly interceptors. Only about 24 A-50s were manufactured in the late 1980s and fewer than a dozen were operational as of 2022, some of them upgraded to the A-50M standard, with a new digital computing system reportedly capable of detecting large aircraft out to a range of 600km and tracking up to 150 targets. Many carried names, like Sergey Atayants in this case, as seen upon arrival in Belarus in early 2022. (Artwork by Tom Cooper)

The most modern tactical fighter-bomber of the VKS to see action against Ukraine in late February and early March 2022 was the Sukhoi Su-35. Jets of this type originally flew escort for ground attack aircraft and helicopter formations of the VKS: due to the expectation of only light resistance, most were relatively lightly armed. This example from the 159th Fighter Aviation Regiment is shown in a typical configuration from this period, including a pair each of Kh-31 anti-radiation missiles (under intakes), R-77-1 medium-range missiles, and R-73 short-range air-to-air missiles. In light of the unexpectedly fierce Ukrainian resistance, as little as two days later Su-35s were observed armed with up to six R-77-1s, two R-73s and two Kh-31s. (Artwork by Tom Cooper)

The principal tactical fighter-bomber of the VKS as of 2022 was the Sukhoi Su-34. Widely propagated as a multi-role jet, in the VKS this type served as the replacement for the obsolete Su-24, and its crews received only a bare minimum of air-to-air training. This example – serial RF-81879 – from the 2nd Guards Composite Aviation Regiment, was shot down over Chernihiv late on 5 March 2022. The crew of two ejected, but only the pilot, Major Aleksander Krasnovartsev survived to become prisoner of war in Ukraine. It is shown as configured when shot down, carrying a total of eight 250kg OFAB-250 bombs. (Artwork by Tom Cooper)

Widely exported through the first two decades of the twenty-first century, and highly praised as one of the most advanced multi-role aircraft in the world, in VKS and Russian Naval Aviation (MA VMF) service the Sukhoi Su-30SM primarily served as an interceptor. During the VSRF advance on Mykolaiv and Voznessensk, jets of this type from the 43rd Independent Naval Assault Aviation Regiment of the MA VMF home-based at Saki in occupied Crimea – armed with Kh-31s, R-27Rs and R-73s, as illustrated here – provided top cover for assault helicopters. Operating deep over Ukrainian-controlled territory with weak electronic warfare support, the unit suffered at least two confirmed losses, apparently both to SA-8s, on 2 and 3 March 2022. (Artwork by Tom Cooper)

As of 2022, the VKS's fleet of Su-25s was down to about 200 aircraft, including around 20 two-seat conversion trainers. Over 100 had been upgraded to the Su-25SM/SM-2/SM-3 standards which – at least nominally – made them compatible with laser-guided weapons like S-25LD rockets, and R-73 air-to-air missiles. Almost all were deployed during the invasion, but usually armed with B-8M or B-13 pods for unguided rockets. This is a reconstruction of the first Su-25 of the VKS known to have been shot down over Ukraine on 24 February 2022. It suffered combat damage from an unknown source while over Ukraine and crashed on Russian territory, killing its pilot as he was attempting to return to base. (Artwork by Tom Cooper)

For much of its early advances into Ukraine, the VSRF depended on its large fleet of Mi-8 assault helicopters. The most advanced of these belonged to a mix of Mi-8AMTSh/-1/-V/-VA variants, manufactured both in Ulan-Ude and Kazan since 2011. These versions are equipped with the Vitebsk self-defence suite (recognisable by the turret installed underneath the cockpit), advanced avionics and a large ramp at the rear, enabling the quicker disembarkation of troops and cargo. This is a reconstruction of the Mi-8AMTSh serial number RF-91165 from the 39th Helicopter Regiment, VKS, home-based at Dzhankoy AB, in occupied Crimea. It was shot down in the Bashtanka area with the loss of five crew and passengers on 2 March 2022. (Artwork by Tom Cooper)

At the start of the invasion in February 2022, all the 30-odd Ukrainian Su-25s were concentrated into the 299th Tactical Aviation Brigade, based at Kulbakyne AB. The fleet had been overhauled and all aircraft repainted in this digital camouflage pattern consisting of four shades of grey, but only seven single-seaters were upgraded to the Su-25M1K standard, including a new fire-control system and head-up display. The unit was rushed into combat early on 25 February, with the task of attacking Russian columns advancing on Kherson. While making repeated strafing runs with S-8 unguided 80mm rockets and their 30mm cannons, three jets – including this example – were shot down by Russian MANPADS: two pilots were killed and the third captured. (Artwork by Tom Cooper)

As of February 2022, the Ukrainian fleet of about 60 MiG-29s was organised into three units: the 114th Brigade in Invano-Frankivsk, the 40th Brigade in Vasylkiv, and the 204th Brigade in Kulbakyne. About a dozen jets had been upgraded to the MiG-29MU1 standard: although highly promising, this was insufficient to significantly change the balance of force vis-à-vis the VKS fleet of MiG-31s, Su-30SMs, and Su-35s. Nevertheless, all three units became involved in numerous combats with enemy aircraft and helicopters, and their pilots claimed numerous aerial victories, leading to the creation of the 'Ghost of Kyiv' legend. Interestingly, whenever deployed against formations of Russian assault helicopters, PSU MiG-29s were armed with B-8M pods for S-8 unguided 80mm rockets, as shown installed on two inboard underwing pylons here. Infrared guided air-to-air missiles, like the R-73M, were apparently not as effective against targets flying very low over the ground. (Artwork by Tom Cooper)

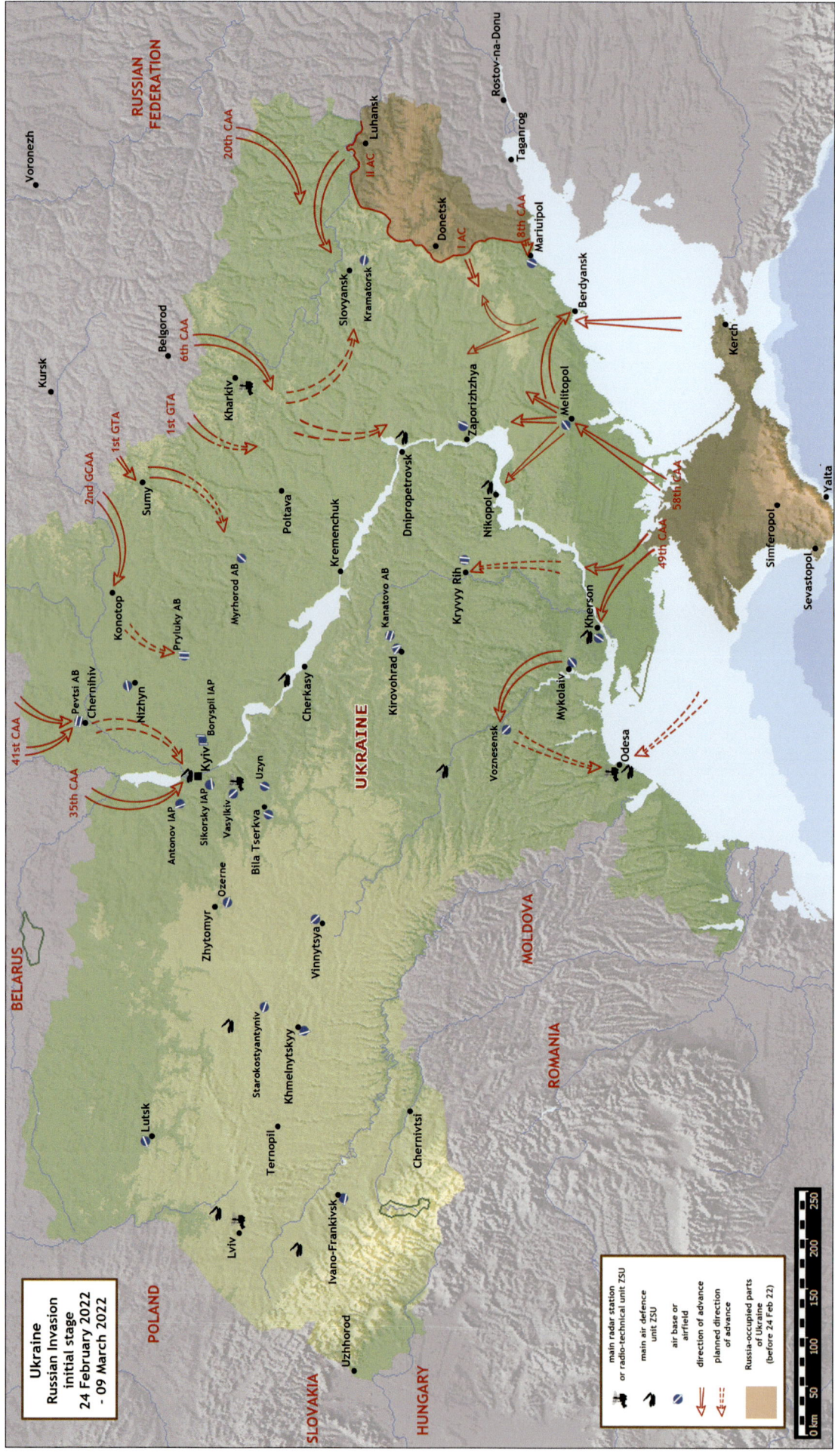

A map of Ukraine with all the main radar stations, air defence units, and air bases of the PSU, and principal directions of the first moves of the Russian invasion of 24 February 2022. (Map by Tom Cooper)

Into the Triangle

The most important element of both the Russian cyber-warfare and anti-radar effort took place in the Kyiv area. Based on a reconstruction of known activities with the help of publicly available information, the conclusion is that the primary aim of both efforts was the creation of an aerial 'safe corridor' necessary for the vital element in the 'coup': an operation aiming to topple the Ukrainian government and thus decapitate and paralyse the military and political leadership of the country, right at the start of the war. As much because of Putin's illusions as the sheer size of the city, and because of Putin's intention to offer his favourites within the VSRF, associated PMCs, and Rosgvardia the opportunity to distinguish themselves, the plan for this enterprise was complex, resulting in a cumbersome and slow execution, and this despite the involvement of too few troops for an operation of this size. It included the infiltration of multiple Spetsnaz and Redut teams into downtown Kyiv, right at the start of the war. Their task was to kill or arrest President Zelensky, members of his cabinet, and his family. In the event of the failure of that mission, two BTGs of airborne troops and one of the Redut PMC were not to assault the Triangle, but to secure airports outside the city, which were to serve as bridgeheads from which additional airborne troops were to advance into the capitol and support the operations of special forces. Hard on their heels, two BTGs of Rosgvardia that were to advance by road all the way from Belarus, and to secure crucial infrastructure facilities around the city, and then wait for the arrival of mechanised units: the latter were to complete the seizure of downtown Kyiv and its isolation from the west and the south.

Battle of Hostomel[5]

Many details of what was going on in Kyiv in the early hours of 24 February 2022 remain obscure: perhaps the most important of the known affairs is that Zelensky was awoken by the call from the commander of the Border Guards, Vitaliy Yavorskiy, who reported that the invasion had begun. The President of Ukraine then set up a meeting of his top advisors and decided to leave the Ministries of Defence and Internal Affairs in Kyiv, but move the rest of his cabinet to western Ukraine, while tasking Colonel General Oleksandr Syrsky with organising the defence of the capital. Figuring out that the Russians would advance along the three major highways from north, west, and east, Syrsky started work on organising two rings of defences: one in the outer suburbs – far enough out to keep the city free from shelling – and one within Kyiv. To establish a clear chain of command, he divided the city into different sectors and appointed generals from military education centres in command of each one. At the time, he had only one regular brigade of the ZSU under command, the 72nd Mechanised (commanded by Colonel Oleksandr Vdovychenko), but military education facilities quickly created several battalions equipped with light weapons, while the 43rd Artillery Brigade added two batteries of 2S7 Pion 203mm self-propelled guns usually used for training.[6]

At dawn, the Russians set in motion their main coup: a BTG of the 31st Guards Airborne Brigade, reinforced by elements of the 45th Spetsnaz Brigade, embarked at least 40 Mi-8 helicopters in southern Belarus, which then flew in a southern direction. Controlled from an Ilyushin Il-20M airborne command post and with the help of at least one A-50, this large and vulnerable formation was escorted by Su-27 and Su-35S interceptors, and Mi-24 and Ka-52 helicopter gunships. It crossed the border while flying down the eastern side of the Dnipro River in the direction of Kyiv.

Unsurprisingly, considering it was carried out in daylight, the operation then encountered fierce resistance. For a start, the ingress of the helicopter formation was detected early, and several Ukrainian interceptors were scrambled in reaction, resulting in several air combats. A number of PSU pilots are known to have fired R-27 air-to-air missiles at incoming helicopters, and a constantly growing number of claims was reported, but the results remain unknown: what is certain is that the escorting Russian interceptors shot down one MiG-29, killing its pilot, Lieutenant Colonel Vyacheslav Yerko, and then a MiG-29UB, the crew of which ejected safely over the Dnipro. Although in some disorder, the Russian helicopter formation continued on to its target. Reaching the area north of the Kyiv Hydroelectric Plant, it turned west to cross the river – and flew straight into the position of several Ukrainian teams equipped with MANPAD systems. At least one Mi-35M was shot down, while one Mi-8AMTSh sustained such damage that it barely managed to reach the Hostomel area before making emergency landings in the fields surrounding Antonov International Airport (AIP): all had to be abandoned by their crews.[7]

Once in the vicinity of the airport, the Russians were much more effective: thanks to the acquisition of precise intelligence provided by the son of an employee at the airport, Ka-52s managed to destroy

A photograph taken on the morning of 24 February 2022 by a Russian airborne soldier of the 31st VDV Brigade. This shows troops and helicopters waiting on a stretch of a road in the Bragin area in southern Belarus, minutes before the start of the heliborne assault on Hostomel. (Ukrainian MOD)

A still from a video showing Russian VDV troops inside an Mi-8 helicopter underway to Antonov IAP early on 24 February 2022. (Ukrainian MOD)

A Konkurs ATGM team of the Russian VDV seen on the streets of Hostomel, early on 24 February 2022. (Russian MOD)

This still from a video shows a pair of Mi-8s underway in the direction of Hostomel, with one of them afire and about to crash. (Ukrainian Internet)

A still from a video showing a single Ka-52 (centre) sheepherding five Mi-8s on the approach to Antonov IAP, as seen from Hostomel. (Ukrainian Internet)

One of several Su-25s of the VKS that attempted to support Russian troops at Antonov IAP, seen passing low over Hostomel. At least two were subsequently claimed as shot down by Ukrainian interceptors. (Ukrainian Internet)

nearly all of the Ukrainian air defences, clearing the way for troop-carrying Mi-8s: only one MANPAD-team of the National Guard fired back at the approaching helicopters, missing once, but then downing the Ka-52 flown by the leader of the Russian formation. On landing at Antonov IAP, the airborne troops quickly fanned out before entrenching themselves around the facility and blocking all the approaches to it.[8]

Disturbed by the loss of strategic communications and repeated air strikes by the Russian Ka-52s, Mi-24s, and Su-25s that caused them significant losses, the Ukrainians were relatively slow to react. Elements of the 72nd Mechanised Brigade, the Hostomel-based 4th Rapid Reaction Brigade of the National Guard (which was still in the process of expansion from a regiment to a brigade, and thus actually understrength for a brigade), and the Alfa Group of the Security Service of Ukraine (*Sluzhba bezpeky Ukrainy*, SBU: the principal security and counterintelligence service of the country) supported by BMP-2s began converging upon Antonov IAP only around noon. They were reinforced by several groups of armed volunteers and 48 paratroopers of the 80th Airborne Assault Brigade, deployed by three Mi-8 helicopters on the south-western side of the airport. Using brief cell phone messages to coordinate their attack, the Ukrainians counterattacked around 16.00hrs: their assault was stopped cold as the troops began suffering losses in the face of heavy Russian fire, while trying to overcome a wall surrounding most of the sprawling installation. Frustrated, the Ukrainians withdrew when they ran out of ammunition, leaving Kyiv to claim the recovery of the IAP around 20.00hrs local time. Actually, most of the 31st Guards Airborne present at the airport did not even see any action: they spent the day expanding their positions around the airport. Nevertheless, the counterattack was effective: it bought the time for Pions deployed by Syrsky north-west of Kyiv to shell the runway, cratering it in several places. The damage was further increased by two Ukrainian Su-24Ms with the use of 500kg runway-cratering bombs at last light, and then by several volleys of artillery fire from the 72nd Mechanised. With this, Antonov IAP was rendered useless to the Russians, and the planned landing of up to 18 Ilyushin Il-76 transports underway from Pskov AB with reinforcements and heavy equipment had to be cancelled. These were rerouted before entering the airspace over northern Ukraine: most likely, they joined about 50 other aircraft of the same type that reportedly landed at Bobruysk AB during the afternoon and evening.

Overall, the Russians remained in control of Antonov IAP, even if it was useless for their purposes and their grip was anything but firm. Four Ukrainian troops were cut off during the withdrawal and managed to hide inside one of numerous buildings of the complex. They were to play a crucial role in the coming days.[9]

Two Pion self-propelled artillery pieces of the 43rd Artillery Brigade rushing through Kyiv to meet the Russian assault in the north-west early on 24 February 2022. (Ukrainian MOD)

Table 9: VSRF Forces in northern Ukraine, February–March 2022

Unit	Known number of BTGs	Comment
35th Combined Arms Army		from OSK East
5th Guards Tank Brigade	2	from 36th CAA (OSK East)
31st Guards Airborne Brigade	1	from VDV
36th Guards Motorised Rifle Brigade	1	from 29th CAA (OSK East)
37th Guards Motorised Rifle Brigade	2	from 36th CAA (OSK East)
38th Guards Motorised Rifle Brigade	1	
45th Guards Spetsnaz	1	
64th Motorised Rifle Brigade	1	
69th Covering Brigade	1	
76th Guards Airborne Division	2	from VDV
98th Guards Airborne Division	4	from VDV
106th Guards Airborne Division	4	from VDV

Chernobyl

Meanwhile, north of Kyiv, the 35th CAA – commanded by Lieutenant General Aleksandr Semyonovich Sanchik – opened its onslaught with a vicious artillery barrage and a few air strikes on known Ukrainian positions between Radcha and Ivankiv. Taken by surprise, the surviving Ukrainian Border Guards – which had only minor units deployed along the border – rapidly withdrew, while the ZSU was nowhere to be found, with one exception. The 177th Battalion National Guard, the unit protecting the Chernobyl nuclear power plant, surrendered to the advancing Russians on the morning of 24 February: over 200 troops went into captivity.

Rushing in a southern direction, late in the afternoon of 24 February 2022, Sanchik's troops reached Ivankiv, a town on the Teteriv River, about 80km north of the centre of Kyiv. The place was quickly secured by a spearhead of Spetsnaz and the North BTG of the Redut PMC, who also captured the crucial bridge on the R02 highway, thus enabling the 35th CAA to push southwards without delay. Sanchik's sole problem at this stage was the fact that all the way between the border with Belarus and Ivankiv, he had only one road at his disposal: the P36 motorway. This meant that he had to array all the units of his army one after the other. Regardless of how fast they could move in theory, in practice even the fastest of his motorised or mechanised units were advancing at the pace of their slowest vehicles and took up lots of space: even if most of 35th CAA's BTGs were not at their full nominal strength, each still included about 100 heavy vehicles. Moreover, each required its support unit of about 20–22 transport vehicles. Under combat conditions, these were required to move spaced by at least 50 metres – better 100 metres – meaning that a single BTG was usually stretched over anything between 5,000 and 10,000 metres of the P36. Once Sanchik's BTGs had – in a long defile, one after the other – reached the R02 highway, individual vehicles still had to keep their security spacing, but were at least capable of advancing simultaneously along at least two lanes, thus shortening the length of each unit to about 2,500–3,000 metres. That said, in their rear, a giant traffic snarl began building up because as additional BTGs rushed into Ukraine they became entangled with the supply vehicles of units that were already well forward. The resulting traffic jam, further increased by the first ambushes set up by armed Ukrainian volunteers, was to significantly contribute to the total collapse of 35th CAA's undertaking.

Fatal Blows

The night from 24 to 25 February 2022 was particularly tense in Kyiv, as not only was large part of the 35th CAA approaching the city along the R02 highway, but several small groups of Russian Spetsnaz, GRU, and PMCs had infiltrated with the aim of attacking the Triangle. Obviously, their efforts were fruitless: mostly repelled by bodyguards and troops of the 1st Operational Brigade: safe inside a deep underground bunker constructed during Soviet times, the President and his cabinet had survived, and promptly began rallying Ukrainians into armed resistance: over the following week, Zelensky was reportedly to survive at least three, perhaps half a dozen additional assassination attempts.[10]

This – fully armed – Su-27 of the Ukrainian Air Force landed at the 95th Air Base of the Romanian Air Force, outside Bacau, early on 24 February 2022 due to pilot disorientation. The aircraft was flown back to Ukraine – disarmed – a few days later. (MaPN)

Wrecked hulks of Kamaz trucks that carried some assailants into downtown Kyiv, seen early on 26 February 2022. (Ukrainian Internet)

The morning of 25 February 2022 began with reports of the Ukrainian air defences engaging targets directly over the city: the S-300-equipped 96th Air Defence Brigade evacuated its base in time to avoid the opening Russian strikes; the 138th Radio-Technical Brigade did not, but although one of its barracks was hit by a cruise missile, 50 troops inside survived. By the morning of 25 February, both units were in position: the 138th was guiding the operations of the 96th, and of MiG-29 and Su-27 interceptors.

Indeed, much of Kyiv was woken up by a spectacular explosion in the dark skies above the city: eventually, it transpired that this was a Su-27 of the PSU. Related Russian reports were not specific enough to enable a conclusion if the jet was shot down in air combat, or by a long-range fire from a VKS S-400 SAM site reportedly deployed about 120 kilometres north of the Ukrainian capital.

If far too many details about the air warfare over Kyiv during the first 48 hours remain obscure, there is little doubt that Sanchik made good use of the first night and the second morning of the war. All the time hurried by Putin, after reaching the R02 highway, early on the 25th he rushed a column of the 45th Spetsnaz and Redut PMC wearing ZSU uniforms, followed by Chechens of the 141st Special Motor Rifle Regiment, straight on to Kyiv. In the village of Demydiv this column split, with the Chechens led by General Maghomed Tushayev assaulting and quickly securing the homebase of the 4th Rapid Reaction Brigade, before linking up with airborne assault troops at Antonov IAP: the latter was not under Ukrainian pressure because early on 25 February, all the ZSU units were ordered to withdraw to a defence line along the Irpin River, completed by Zaluzhny's order, 'Not one step back'.

Meanwhile, the balance of the Spetsnaz and Redut's North BTG pressed towards Kyiv: due to poor coordination, they took each other under fire while exiting southern Demydiv along two parallel roads, and the mercenaries suffered heavy losses. After sorting themselves out, both columns regrouped and pushed southwards again. Although delayed, their appearance took the defenders by surprise and it was only once the leading Russian vehicles reached the Saint Sophia Cathedral – on the northern fringe of the 'Triangle' – that they were stopped. There followed a series of bitter, but chaotic, short-range firefights through the Piorka and then Vysihorod districts, in which most of the Russian vehicles were knocked out and dozens of assailants killed. Simultaneously, another attack – unclear if by Spetsnaz or Redut – targeted the Kyiv Hydroelectric Plant: eventually, it took the deployment of the Ukrainian Alfa Group SBU to force the assailants away during the evening of 25 February.

Later during the morning, Ukrainian sappers blew up a bridge carrying the R02 highway across the Irpin River south of Demydiv, and a part of the dam near the village of Kozarovychi: this caused wholesale flooding of the area between Dnipro in the north down to Irpin, thus blocking the direct approach to the Ukrainian capital. If he wanted to continue advancing with the 35th CAA, Sanchik was now forced to find an indirect route.

35th CAA on E40

The loss of R02, the two failed forays into Kyiv, and much stronger Ukrainian resistance than expected seems to have sealed the fate of the Russian assault on the Triangle before it had even begun. Nevertheless, kicked and pushed by Putin all the time, Sanchik continued ordering his units into further assaults, as soon as they

A pair of BTR-82s of the Rosgvardia's 141st Special Motor Rifle Regiment, entirely staffed by Chechens, seen during their march on Ivankiv, late in the afternoon of 24 February 2022.

Ukrainian Mi-24PU1 seen attacking the advancing Russians in the area of Antonov IAP early on 25 February 2022. (Ukrainian Inernet)

the Chechens were ambushed and then almost completely destroyed by Ukrainian artillery, losing more than 50 vehicles and General Tushayev in the process, on 26 February.[11]

Undaunted by reports about losses and growing supply problems, Putin kept on pushing, and thus Sanchik made his next move on the morning of 27 February, by when additional BTGs of airborne troops had reached the Demydiv area, followed by the first mechanised forces. Sanchik thus ordered a multi-BTG push, but this time from the R02 in a south-western direction, with his western flank advancing via Borodyanka (which had a small civilian airport nearby) on Makariv, the central via Bucha and Vorzel on Mykolaivka or Buzova – all three villages along the E40/M06 highway connecting Kyiv with Zhytomir; and the eastern on the village of Moshchun.

Already short on infantry, the 35th now had to advance with mechanised formations through densely built-up areas full of civilians that were informing the ZSU about its every move, while being repeatedly ambushed by small Ukrainian units well-equipped with anti-tank weapons, constrained to roads by the soft ground, and lacking a clear idea about precise enemy positions. In other words: Putin forced Sanchink and his 35th CAA to operate against the fundamentals of the VSRF doctrine.

'Orders are orders', and thus the involved units pressed on and by the afternoon of 27 February the western flank of the 35th CAA had not only passed Borodyanka but drove all the way to Makariv. Following the standard doctrine, instead of entering the village – at the time defended by just 80 Ukrainian troops – the Russian motor rifle troops mounted on BMP-2s and BTR-82s moved around it, shooting up any civilian cars passing by as they went, killing dozens. By the morning of 28 February, they had blocked the E40/M06 south of Makariv before actually assaulting and securing the village a day later.

The central flank of this advance – consisting of a BTG of the 331st Airborne Regiment – was nowhere near as successful: as the spearhead, including about a dozen armoured vehicles, entered Bucha and drove down Vokzalna Street in a long defile, it was ambushed by elements of the 72nd Airborne and several groups of volunteers. After a pitched battle lasting three hours, the Russian column was destroyed and the few survivors scattered in all directions.[12]

However, it was the Moshchun area that proved the biggest problem for Sanchink and his troops. Situated east of the Irpin delta, a dense forest dotted by bunkers from the Second World War was held by a battalion of the 72nd Mechanised and stopped the Russian river-crossing cold.

Meanwhile, another column of Russian military vehicles came down the R02 and then turned right in Demydiv, before reaching Antonov IAP: this included the heavy equipment of the 31st

came down the R02 from Ivankyiv. By then, the 72nd Mechanised had been significantly reinforced by a growing number of armed volunteers, many of whom possessed extensive combat experience from the Donbass over the last eight years. Thus, when the BTG 141st Special Motor Rifle Regiment was ordered to reach Kyiv by advancing via Bucha and Irpin without sufficient reconnaissance, it drove straight into a catastrophe: shortly after entering Bucha,

A BMD-2 of a VDV unit in the Hostomel area on 26 or 27 February 2022. (Ukrainian Internet)

Two columns of vehicles of the 31st Airborne Assault Brigade, seen approaching their refuelling point at Antonov IAP, shortly before the Ukrainian artillery barrage of 27 February. (Ukrainian MOD)

When the fires had burned out, only charred wreckage remained of the 31st Airborne Assault Brigade. Notable in the centre is the Mriya Hangar with the wreckage of the An-225. (Ukrainian MOD)

– and several reconnaissance UAVs. As the Russian vehicles converged in long columns upon the refuelling point, they were subjected to a massive artillery barrage of Syrkyn's 2S7s and the 72nd Mechanised Brigade's artillery. In a matter of minutes, the majority of vehicles of the 31st Airborne Assault Brigade, and about 60 of its troops were destroyed – but so was also the sole operational Antonov An-225 Mriya, the biggest transport aircraft in the world.

Regardless of another catastrophic loss, or perhaps because he was not keen to forward bad news to Moscow, Sanchik remained under pressure from Putin. Therefore, he continued trying and ordered the second BTG of the 31st Airborne – a unit that spent the first three days of the war securing Antonov IAP – to take over vehicles from the 11th Airborne Assault Brigade and – as soon as possible – take Bucha, and then advance on Kyiv. Unsurprisingly considering the hurry in which this attack was launched, it ended in another catastrophe. After entering Bucha, the second BTG of the 31st Airborne Assault Brigade was ambushed by Ukrainian infantry, which then called in another artillery strike. By the time the battle was over, only two Russian soldiers survived to tell the story, and both of them – including the deputy commander of the brigade – were captured.[13]

Still, the ultimate result of the first phase of the 35th CAA's advance on Kyiv was a stalemate: multiple Russian BTGs were destroyed; several were mauled and down to their last troops; while others were strewn all the way from Moshchun in the north-east, via Bucha to Makariv in the south, and entangled in a labyrinth of villages along the northern bank of the Irpin River. However, they had managed to block the E40/M06. On the other hand, the Ukrainian defences, centred on the 72nd Mechanised but largely consisting of armed volunteers, were most of the time critically short of ammunition. Sanchik's 35th CAA thus appeared to be on

Airborne Assault Brigade. After a long march from the border with Belarus all the vehicles needed refuelling. For this purpose, the Russians grouped them in between the Mriya and Antonov hangars, where they were expected to remain invisible to Ukrainian artillery observers on the ground. However, they were perfectly visible to the four Ukrainian special forces operators cut off since 24 February the verge of accomplishing at least the task of isolating Kyiv from western Ukraine through continuing its advance in a southern direction.

Assaults on Sikorsky International Airport and Vasylkiv AB

Antonov Airport was one of four or five airports the Russians – reportedly – intended to capture in the first hours of their invasion: their other aims might have been Borsypil International (south-east of Kyiv), Sviatoshyn Airport (western Kyiv), Sikorsky International (south-western Kyiv, also known as Zhulyany), and Vasylkiv Air Base (40km south-west of Kyiv). As described above, the assault on Sviatoshyn was eventually undertaken by the 35th CAA, but ended in the destruction of the BTG in question. The assault on Boryspil appears to have been abandoned. Strangely enough, the assaults on Sikorsky International and on Vasylkiv AB were undertaken, nevertheless, resulting in a series of engagements that largely remain obscure.

On 25 February, General Serhii Kryvonos – former Deputy Commander of the Special Operation Forces, and then the Deputy Secretary of the National Security and Defence Council of Ukraine, dismissed by President Zelensky from the ZSU in 2019 – arrived at Sikorsky International to find it 'held' by a few small groups of the Border Guards and the National Guard, and a few cadets from the Taras Shevchenko National University in Kyiv. According to his own recollections, Kryvonos then assumed command upon his own initiative and developed a plan for defence – bolstered by the arrival of a composite unit consisting of veterans of the Right Sector that he had called for help. Obstacles were deployed up and down the runway to prevent a possible landing by Russian transport aircraft, then it was mined, and finally the defenders took up carefully selected positions: just in time, for the Russians appeared just hours later.[14]

In the early hours of 26 February, an air raid alert was sounded in the Kyiv area, and a Su-27 interceptor of the Ukrainian Air Force, piloted by Colonel Oleksander Mostovoy scrambled in that direction. Eventually, Mostovoy claimed to have intercepted an Il-76 transport just as it was about to disgorge VDV troops upon Sikorsky International, and shot it down. Whether the large, jet-powered transport was really shot down remains unclear: the Ukrainians never showed any kind of evidence for this claim. Nevertheless, according to Kryvonos, about 20 Russian troops managed to jump out, and they were quickly eliminated by Ukrainian ground troops.

Meanwhile, the Ukrainians claimed another Il-76 as shot down by their air defences over the Bila Tserkva area, and then also the downing of two helicopters a few kilometres outside Vasylkiv: nevertheless – at least according to the Ukrainian sources, the Russians still managed to land enough troops at this air base to press home their attack. This was repelled by the Ukrainians at a cost of about 30 casualties, including 10 defenders killed. By the evening of 26 February, surviving Russian airborne troops withdrew into the forests of the Plesetske area.[15]

With this, by the end of the third day of the war, the VSRF had managed to secure one airport in the Kyiv area – Antonov – but this was useless for further action, and it had clearly failed to either enter, or at least encircle, the Ukrainian capital.

6
CITY FORTRESSES

If the 35th CAA had managed to rush all the way down from the border with Belarus into the north-western outskirts of Kyiv without much ado before encountering serious resistance, nothing similar can be said about the 41st CAA. Tasked with securing the Chernihiv Oblast, in north-eastern Ukraine, and then continuing to Kyiv, right from the start of the war, and for the next two weeks, it experienced one catastrophe after another.

Collapse of the 41st CAA

Commanded by Lieutenant General Sergey Ryzhkov, the 41st CAA crossed the border and converged on Chernihiv along two highways, the E95 in the west, and the P13 in the east. While Putin, Shoygu, and Gerasimov might have expected Ryzhkov's troops to have it easy in accomplishing this mission, the subsequent operations of the 41st CAA fully exposed all of their failures and illusions.

Just a few dozen kilometres into Ukraine, Ryzhkov's units began losing troops and vehicles for all possible reasons: most had never been informed that they were going into a war but were told that they were about to participate in a four-day-long exercise. Next, the communication system of the 41st CAA collapsed because it was based on a Russian GSM system, which did not work in Ukraine. Troops looted local shops for Ukrainian SIM cards, in turn enabling Ukrainian COMINT-gathering units to read their communications in clear – only to quickly find out the Russian spearheads experienced massive problems while trying to reach any of their commanders. Finally, operated by disgruntled troops forced to live on 'meals, ready to eat' that had long since expired, vehicles poorly maintained for years before the war broke down or ran out of fuel and were then abandoned. Constantly adding salt to the self-inflicted injuries of the 41st CAA were the 'technoguerrilla' tactics of the dozens of small Ukrainian volunteer units facing it. Instead of operating in large concentrations, the Ukrainians roamed main roads in squads of 8 to 15 troops, armed with ATGMs, anti-material and sniper rifles, and mounted on high-mobility vehicles. Up to a dozen of such squads usually operated along each of the highways used by the Russians to advance, most supported by mini-UAVs, sometimes by BRDM-2 armoured scout cars that constantly tracked the enemy movement. Whenever a suitable position was found, the squad would either mine a portion of the road, or bring its ATGM into position, knock out one or more Russian vehicles from a range of 2,000 or more metres, and then promptly withdraw at its best speed. The number of such squads and the speed of their manoeuvre was usually such that even their own commanders had no clear idea where exactly the units were, and, obviously, not all of their ambushes were successful. However, by knocking out several vehicles from each of the Russian BTGs they ran into, they began rapidly draining the combat power of the 41st CAA, and ruining the morale of its troops – and that well before the 41st had approached Chernihiv. Worst of all were their ambushes of logistic convoys, which regularly left entire columns of trucks afire, further worsening

A Russian T-72B knocked out in a clash with the 1st Tank Brigade on the approaches to Chernihiv on 26 February 2022. (Ukrainian MOD)

the supply situation of Ryzhkov's undersupplied and disgruntled troops. The unavoidable consequence was that within only two to three days of operations, much of the 41st CAA effectively fell apart: not only were troops hungry, cold and isolated, but many were shocked when suffering severe losses to Ukrainian resistance and some – like an entire reconnaissance platoon of the 74th Guards Motor Rifle Brigade – surrendered without a fight. Hundreds of others abandoned their vehicles and fled back towards Belarus. Obviously, this bought plenty of time for the Ukrainians to improve their positions further to the rear.

The centrepiece of the ZSU in that part of the country was the 1st Tank Brigade, home-based in Honsharivske, on the northern verge of the giant nature reserve of Mizrichvisnkyi. The unit had already taken positions around Chernihiv, carefully evacuated and concealed its ammunition and food stocks before the invasion and was constantly kept updated on the enemy advance once this began. Nevertheless, considering the quantitative and qualitative superiority of the 41st CAA in numbers and firepower, it might appear as 'bordering on a miracle' that the Ukrainian brigade was not, literally, pulverised in the first few days of the war. Instead, in its first known action, the 1st Tank quickly brought the advance of Ryzhkov's troops to a halt in the Sednev area, by destroying numerous vehicles – including a better part of a battery of BM-21 multiple rocket launchers – early on 25 February. As the chaos continued to spread within units of the 41st CAA, Ryzhkov rushed his deputy, Major General Andrey Sukhovetsky, to the front: where he was shot by a Ukrainian sniper on 28 February. Eventually, it took the Russian army commander several days longer to regain control and reorganise the 41st CAA sufficiently enough to launch a serious push on Chernihiv. Even then, a week later, he lost his Chief-of-Staff and second deputy, Major General Vitaly Gerasimov, killed on 7 March.

Table 10: VSRF Units in North-Eastern Ukraine, February 2022		
Unit	Number of BTGs	Notes
41st Combined Arms Army		OSK Centre; about 14 BTGs as of 23 February
35th Guards Motorised Rifle Brigade	2	
55th Motorised Rifle Brigade	2	
74th Guards Motorised Rifle Brigade	2	
90th Tank Division	4	from OSK Centre

Shostka, Konotop and Sumy

The task of securing north-eastern Ukraine was assigned to the 2nd Guards Combined Arms Army of the VSRF. Although disturbed by similar problems to the 41st CAA, fewer than a dozen BTGs of this army had advanced fast enough to surround both Shostka in the north and the town of Konotop in the south, by the morning of 25 February. However, they had too few troops and were in too much of a rush to secure anything at all: indeed, the first Russian attack into Konotop was, reportedly, smashed by the ZSU garrison there, with a loss of about 40 vehicles of all types. Eventually, the 2nd GCAA proved unable to exercise control not only over this town, but even over the E101/M02 highway: all the time losing vehicles to mechanical breakdowns and lack of fuel, it was subjected to numerous ambushes set up by the Ukrainians and began falling apart.

Further south, the spearheads of the 'crack' 1st Guards Tank Army (1st GTA) – including (arrayed from north to south) multiple BTGs of the 27th Guards Motor Rifle Brigade, the famous 2nd Guards Tamanskaya Motor Rifle Division (best known for its

TECHNOGUERRILLA[1]

The Russian invasion – and especially the onslaught on Antonov IAP and the rush of the 35th CAA on Kyiv – caught the ZSU in the process of mobilisation. While delaying actions by special forces and logistical mishaps did slow down the Russian advance, the capital was initially defended by only two significant units, both from the National Guard: the 1st Operational Brigade, tasked with protection of the President, and the 4th Rapid Reaction Brigade, based in Hostomel. Theoretically, the Ukrainians could call upon the 112th TD Brigade, home-based in Kyiv, but as of 24 February, this was a cadre formation and took several days to fully mobilise. Therefore, the General Staff of the ZSU reacted to the Russian attack by ordering the 72nd Mechanised Brigade from Bila Tserkva, the 95th Airborne Assault Brigade from Zhytomyr, 14th Mechanised Brigade from Volodymyr, the 26th Artillery Brigade from Berdychiv, and the 43rd Artillery Brigade from Divychki to converge on the capitol. Even then, this did not trigger some sort of major showdown of mechanised formations, as expected by many. Amid the general chaos of the first few days of war, the Ukrainians operate in a completely unforeseen way: as 'technoguerrillas'. These tactics came into being through a process of trial and error and a number of distinct factors.

The foremost issue was the local geography, consisting of large forests and swamps, intersected by several rivers, and criss-crossed by urban and semi-urban areas. While tying the Russian mechanised formations to the roads, this favoured infantry combat, even more so in the adverse weather of late February and early March. In this regard, the situation only worsened once the Ukrainians had blown up several bridges on the Irpin River and then the dam in Demydiv, flooding a large area north-west of Kyiv.

The second important factor was that a large number of Ukrainian volunteers took matters into their own hands. Many reached the frontline in their own private vehicles, and most were combat experienced: some acted entirely on their own, others joined several special forces units to engage the advancing Russian columns without waiting for detailed instructions or orders. The result was the creation of many very small, yet highly mobile units, mostly of squad or platoon-size. The Ukrainians quickly learned not only to make use of the latest Western-supplied ATGMs like NLAW and Javelin, but to roam the battlefield around the roads used by the Russians, plant mines, and conduct hit-and-run attacks, or set up ambushes and to call up artillery strikes. Within only two or three days, the battlefield thus become an apparent chaos of ambushes, strikes from close and afar, in which the VSRF was suffering massive losses. Certainly enough, while undergoing the trial and error process, the Ukrainians suffered losses, primarily to Russian 30mm autocannons installed on BMP-2, BMP-3, BMD-3, and BMD-4 infantry fighting vehicles, and on BTR-82 armoured personnel carriers. However, their 'technoguerrilla' tactics soon proved effective to the degree where regular ZSU units began applying them too, eventually switching into an extreme form of the *Auftragstaktik*, in which brigade commanders were only able to issue very general instructions, but the bulk of decision-making took place at the level below that of company commander. In turn, this was why the Ukrainians deployed their heavy weapons only sparingly: tanks, for example, usually operated in pairs, as assault guns providing fire-support, and then withdrawn as soon as possible. More often, the combat proven Kropyva Automatic Tactical Management System (ATMS; see below for details) enabled the Ukrainians to integrate information provided by their technoguerrillas and by civilian observers behind the enemy lines, from Ukrainian and allied Western intelligence services, and UAVs, with the fire actions of their artillery. This combination was eventually to prove murderously effective, as summarised by a Ukrainian officer: '…anti-tank mines have slowed the Russians down, but what killed them was our artillery'.

The technoguerrilla tactics caught the Russians entirely unprepared: indeed, in the worst possible position to deal with the combination of continuous ambushes and artillery barrages. Tied down to the roads and their vehicles, without knowledge of the local terrain, and rarely supported even by their own forward artillery observers, the VRSF units proved unable to follow developments on a highly fluid battlefield. Moreover, as was soon to become obvious: they were not only lacking intelligence but were demoralised and critically short on supplies.

A Russian BMP-2 knocked out in one of many ambushes on the approach to Sumy in early March 2022. (Ukrainian MOD)

regular appearances at the May Day parades in Red Square in Moscow), the 47th Guards Tank Division, and the famed 4th Guards Kantemirovskaya Tank Division – had entered Sumy Oblast without encountering much resistance. There is still a sizeable dose of uncertainty regarding the 1st GTA's objectives, with most of sources pointing at Kyiv but some in the direction of Cherkasy or Poltava.

Certainly enough, troops of the 27th Division appeared in downtown Sumy around noon on 24 February, experiencing more problems with traffic snarls than with Ukrainian

Typical scenes of the early days of the Russian advance into Ukraine across all areas: poorly maintained vehicles that suffered mechanical breakdowns, or had run out of fuel, had to be towed in order for the advance to continue. Dozens and then hundreds were simply abandoned, many others destroyed in Ukrainian ambushes. (Ukrainian Internet)

resistance: only some 50 paratroopers of the ZSU were in the city. In the evening, they ambushed and destroyed a column of Russian tanks near the art college, but were subsequently withdrawn, together with most of the police and much of city's leadership. However, the Russians then made a crucial mistake: in their rush towards Kyiv and Cherkasy, their spearhead merely drove through Sumy, without securing any of the important installations. The follow-up units were delayed, leaving the confused and shocked locals to organise the city's defences on their own. Although only about 20 out of the 400 that gathered that afternoon had previous military experience, they armed themselves with assault rifles and anti-tank weapons found in an abandoned military base, and then coordinated via social media. In the course of several short-range engagements during the following night, they destroyed enough of enemy vehicles to convince the Russians to remain outside Sumy. For the rest of February and into early March, the heavily mechanised but completely disorganised and poorly commanded 1st GTA was busy extracting its tanks and other vehicles from the mud, where these became struck while trying to bypass the city. Sumy thus remained safely in Ukrainian hands and was soon to prove a major thorn in the side of the Russian onslaught.[2]

The situation on the roads used by the 41st CAA and the 1st GTA for their attempts to advance eventually worsened to degree where the VKS had to deploy its attack helicopters – like this Ka-52 – to carry out reconnaissance in front of every convoy of VSRF vehicles. (Russian MOD)

Kharkiv

The onslaught of the 6th CAA on Kharkiv began at 04.58hrs on 24 February 2022, with a number of red flares rising into the dark sky over the border. There followed the usual, vicious volleys of artillery and multiple rocket launchers at the nearest Ukrainian positions – which were as empty as those in the north. By 06.00hrs, long columns of VSRF vehicles were flowing over the border. As far as can be said, the ZSU units in front did not simply flee, but conducted a fighting withdrawal: in one of the first clashes on the E105/M20 highway, five to six kilometres south of Mitnitsya, troops of the 92nd Mechanised Brigade knocked out a Tigr MRAP waving the Ukrainian flag, a

BMP-2, and an MT-LB, having one BTR-4 damaged in return. Taken by surprise, and having several of their vehicles stuck in the mud, the Russians regrouped and then continued their advance, only to run into another ambush in which at least three MBTs and several MT-LBs were destroyed. Once again, the Russians repeated the exercise of regrouping, before continuing their advance down the M02 – straight into the next ambush: by the time the spearhead of the 6th CAA Derhachi and Lisne, it had lost more than two dozen armoured fighting vehicles, in return knocking out perhaps two or three Ukrainian. By the evening, the 6th CAA was already lagging badly behind its plan to surround Kharkiv.

The situation was similar to the north-east of the second largest city of Ukraine, where the at least five BTGs of the 144th Motor Rifle Division of the 20th CAA rushed to capture Ternova before continuing for Staryi Saltiv and the nearby dam spanning the Siversky Donets River, pending further advances south and south-west of Kharkiv. Following not only their doctrine, but also the battle plan, the VSRF units did not attempt to drive straight into downtown Kharkiv, but split and continued to the east, south, and west – around the city – as described by a battalion commander of the 92nd Mech:

> Our main task was to hold Kharkiv and prevent the enemy from entering the city. As we later found out, after capturing their documentation and maps, the enemy was tasked with encircling the city using motorised infantry units. They had information that there were no troops in Kharkiv, only minor militia. That's what they called the 92nd Brigade…. On the 24th they were to cross the border, on the 25th to set up an outer circle around the city, on the 26th they were to impose a blockade, and on the 27th their special forces were to enter the centre and capture vital facilities. They expected that Ukrainians would not know what to do, everybody would be fleeing, pro-Russian forces would organise rallies, raise the Russian flag – and voila: they could quickly rule Kharkiv. It all went wrong.[3]

By the end of 24 February, all the Russian units rushing to encircle Kharkiv had suffered severe losses and massive delays. The following morning, the much praised 'elite' of the VSR, the 200th Motor Rifle Brigade then failed to reach and cut off the M03 highway connecting Kharkiv with Poltava. Under rather ironic circumstances, something similar happened to the 144th Motor Rifle Division, east of the city. On the morning of 25 February, the western-most BTG of this division reached the north-western outskirts of Kharkiv in between Shestakove and Kutuzivka and cut off the T2104 road. In this fashion, the Russians blocked the retreat route of the 2nd Battalion of the 92nd Mechanised Brigade, which was withdrawing from Stary Saltiv. Finding no way out of this predicament, the Ukrainian unit – spearheaded by the 6th Company – attempted to pass through the centre of the Russian BTG without opening fire. They were recognised by the enemy while less than 100 metres away: the result was a bitter contest at short range, in which the Ukrainians destroyed 25 enemy armoured fighting vehicles, including at least two MBTs, about a company each of BTR-80s and Tigr MRAPs, and more than 30 trucks, at the price of six of their own BTR-4s and one Dozor-B MRAP.[4] This heavy loss to the 144th, and strong Ukrainian resistance on the approaches to Chuhiv, prevented the 20th CAA from closing the encirclement of Kharkiv from the east and south-east.

Nevertheless, continuously pushed by Putin, commanders of that army and the 6th CAA continued their operation for securing Kharkiv precisely according to the original plan. Although the encirclement and blockade of the city had failed, after two days of preparations, on the morning of 27 February 2022, a long column

Part of a column of the 144th Motor Rifle Division, seen following a short-range clash with the 2nd Battalion, 92nd Mechanised Brigade, on 25 February. (Ukrainian MOD)

A still from a video showing mine-resistant ambush protected vehicles of the 2nd Spetsnaz Regiment, GRU, after their column was ambushed in the outskirts of Kharkiv on 27 February 2022. (Ukrainian MOD)

Table 11: VSRF Forces in eastern Ukraine, February–March 2022		
Unit	Number of BTGs	Notes
2nd Guards Combined Arms Army		from OSK Centre; at least 9 BTGs as of 23 February 2022
15th Guards Motorised Rifle Brigade	2	
138th Guards Motorised Rifle Brigade	1 or 2	from 6th CAA (OSK West)
1st Guards Tank Army		OSK West
27th Motorised Rifle Brigade	3	
200th Motorised Rifle Brigade	2	from XIV Corps (Northern Fleet and Arctic OSK)
2nd Guards Motorised Rifle Division	6	
4th Guards Tank Division	8	
47th Guards Tank Division	5	Newly established unit (2022), from the former 6th Tank Brigade
6th Combined Arms Army		OSK West; at least 11 BTGs as of 23 February 2022
25th Guards Motorised Rifle Brigade	1	
138th Guards Motorised Rifle Brigade	2	
2nd Guards Motorised Rifle Division	2	from 1st Guards Tank Army
144th Motorised Rifle Division	6	from 20th CAA
20th Guards Combined Arms Army		OSK West
3rd Motorised Rifle Division	5	
8th Combined Arms Army		OSK South; at least 8 BTGs as of 23 February 2022
150th Motorised Rifle Division	5–8	
II Army Corps		4 brigades and 1 motor rifle regiment, 1 artillery brigade from LPR
I Army Corps		5 brigades, 1 motor rifle regiment, 1 artillery brigade from DPR

of the 25th Guards Motor Rifle Brigade, reinforced by Spetsnaz troops of the GRU, entered Kharkiv from three directions: Lisopark, Oleksiyivka, and from Tsyrkuny down Shevchenko Street. By this time, the defenders were ready, even if few: they consisted of the 3rd Brigade National Guard on the perimeter, with the 92nd Mech, and a detachment each of Cord and Omega SOF further to the rear. After patiently waiting for the Russians to drive deeper into the city, the Ukrainians counterattacked from multiple directions: by the afternoon, most of the Spetsnaz and an entire BTG of the 25th Guards Motor Rifle Brigade was annihilated, with only a few dozens of survivors managing to escape towards the north.[5]

With this, the Russians had failed to secure at least a part of the second largest city in Ukraine: although remaining in its northern and north-eastern outskirts for a while longer, they were never to attempt a direct attack again.

7
LINE OF CONTROL

Early on 24 February 2022, elements of the 20th CAA and the 8th CAA crossed the international border to enter the areas controlled by the so-called 'Luhansk People's Republic' and the 'Donetsk People's Republic' since 2014–2015, thus re-igniting the war in this part of Ukraine.

Mobilisation in the DPR and the LPR
Despite the huge build-up of Russian forces along the borders of Ukraine, the force posture of the DPR and the LPR did not markedly change. For example, as late as 18 February 2022, there was little reported in regards of a large number of armoured fighting vehicles stored in rearward bases. Nevertheless, both the DPR and the LPR evidently received pre-warning of Putin's plans, as Denis Pushilin, leader of the DPR, announced a general mobilisation on the same day, with the LPR following a day later. Simultaneously, all men between the age of 18 and 55 were prohibited from leaving either of the two self-proclaimed republics, although Moscow pompously announced a 'humanitarian evacuation' of their population, supposedly to avoid an attempt of the ZSU to retake Donbass by force. By 21 February, the police were reportedly collecting young people on the streets of Donetsk into forced conscription.

The mobilisation had a huge effect upon the population of the DPR and LPR, resulting in a very high rate of males being conscripted – even more so considering the sharp reduction in population in these areas since the start of the conflict in 2014. Notably, nothing similar happened in Russia, where Putin did everything in his powers to avoid a mobilisation. The situation reached a point where some senior commanders in the DPR questioned the utility of such conscription and pushing people with minimal training into combat against a generally well-trained and equipped ZSU.[1]

LPR Forces on the Siversky Donets
The exact sequence of the opening stages of the new war in Donbas of 2022 is still unclear. Both the DPR and the LPR issued bombastic

A map of eastern Ukraine with so-called LPR and DPR, the Line of Control, and opening Russian advances. (Map by Tom Cooper)

announcements, and generally proved highly optimistic about their early advances, mirroring the Russian overconfidence about how quickly the campaign would be over. In turn, official Ukrainian sources were largely silent about the developments in this part of the country and the rapid loss of several towns: obviously, all of their attention was directed towards the Russian advance on Kyiv and Kharkiv. Indeed, even the officers and other ranks of ZSU units deployed along the LOC were holding their breath. The battle for Kyiv, and the Russian advances in the Kharkiv area were decisive for their fate: if one of two cities fell, they would have been left with no option but to withdraw towards the Dnipro River.

In Luhansk Oblast, 24 February 2022 began with the authorities announcing that the Ukrainian armed forces had made several attempts to cross the Siversky Donets River, but 'had been repulsed', and that the LPR had now launched a counteroffensive. This narrative fitted well with the overall messaging of the LPR and the neighbouring para-state in the south, both of which had been 'warning' their population of an impending Ukrainian offensive for over a month.

Indeed, early that morning it was the LPR that began its assault, crossing the Siversky Donets at several points in between major Ukrainian fortifications on the LOC. They immediately ran into deep minefields on the northern bank and experienced such problems while trying to pass these, that an advisor to the head of the LPR noted the Separatist troops would not have an easy time with the task.[2] The situation was slightly different at Shchastia, where the ZSU constructed a heavily fortified strongpoint around the old bridge on the M21 highway: the town had been cut off from electricity by Separatist shelling a few days earlier, but Ukrainian units deployed along the Siversky Donets – the 24th Mechanised and the 57th Motor Rifle – easily repelled the first waves of enemy attacks. It was only once it became obvious that the VSRF was in the process of invading northern Luhansk, that a decision had to be taken to withdraw. The advance of the 20th CAA was threatening to drive straight into their rear and isolate them from the rest of Ukraine. Following a phased withdrawal from the bridgehead, the bridge was demolished on 28 February.[3]

Although the crossing attempt at Shchastia was thwarted, the LPR forces eventually managed to create bridgeheads elsewhere. Apparently, the first of these came into being about 16km south-west of Shchastia, near the village of Lopaskyne, and enabled the construction of a pontoon bridge that was operational by the end of 24 February. However, deep minefields then limited the further advance to only about 1,500 metres. Further east, the Separatists took Stanytsia Luahnska almost without resistance, and then launched the construction of another bridge: two days later, LPR militants posted photographs of themselves inside the local administration buildings and while removing Ukrainian flags and other symbols.[4]

The third major crossing point became Trokhizbenka, around 20km west of Shchastia, where a narrow bridge carrying a minor road still spanned the Siversky Donets. While the Russian sources claimed that Trokhizbenka was captured on the first day of attacks, the Ukrainians stressed that the initial LPR assault had been repulsed with the loss of two MBTs and one IFV operated by Separatists. Although the exact date remains unclear, the village was secured by the Ghost Battalion of the LPR on 25 February, where the Separatists captured one of first US-made FGM-148 Javelin anti-tank systems. With this, and although being held-up at Shchastia, the LPR forces had crossed the Siversky Donets and then launched an advance in the western direction. The way for the conquest of the whole Luhansk Oblast was open for the Russians and the Separatists alike, and the VSRF was now free to avoid attempting to penetrate the heavily fortified LOC and try to drive around its northern flank.[5]

It was under these conditions that the Russians secured the heavily fortified second-line Ukrainian position constructed on commanding heights overlooking the P22 highway about six kilometres north of Stanytsia Luhanska, in the suburb of Makarove, on 28 February, and then reached Svatove and the outskirts of Rubizhne, north of Severodonetsk, on 1 March 2022, where they were held by elements of the 24th Mechanised and the 57th Motor Rifle brigades of the ZSU. Two days later, the Russian and LPR forces met in Novoaidr, 30km northwest of Shchastia, in a highly publicised event. Most likely, the first actual such meeting took place at least two days earlier, and further to the north-west.[6] By 4 March, elements of the 20th CAA, combined with the LPR forces that operated as the I Army Corps, were approaching the large urban conurbations of Severodonetsk, Lysychansk, and Rubizhne, but then swung around them to enter the north-eastern part of the Donetsk Oblast, and capture several villages about 20km north-east of Sloviansk.

Flanking LOC from the South
On 24 February 2022, in the Donetsk Oblast, the DPR commenced the assault with two major offensive thrusts. The first originated from the vicinity of the Separatist-controlled village of Petrivske, and struck west across the LOC, towards the town of Volnovakha, a strategically important location about 25km away from the M20 highway connecting Donetsk with Mariupol and held by the 56th Motor Rifle Brigade of the ZSU. The aim of this effort was to reach Pokrovsk. The second main effort was in the south, along the coast of the Azov Sea, directly towards Mariupol, where the DPR forces advanced in cooperation with the 150th Motor Rifle Division, VSRF.

On 24 February, Eduard Basurin, the official spokesman of the DPR, had announced that the armed forces of the para-state were reaching the pre-2014 administrative boundaries of the Donetsk Oblast. In reality, on the first day, the DPR units did manage to breach the Ukrainian defence lines but advanced by only about three kilometres, suffering heavy losses while capturing the small village Bohdanivka on their way to Volnovakha. Two days later, the DPR forces were still outside Volnovakha, but the town was under constant shelling. That said, either on 26 or 27 February, the 11th Motor Rifle Regiment of the DPR – supported by the 163rd Tank Regiment of the 150th Motor Rifle Division, VSRF – did manage to reach the M20 highway south of Volnovakha, thus cutting off the primary land connection to Mariupol.[7]

In the south, the DPR and the VSRF advanced slightly faster, primarily because the chief of the police of Mariupol, and a large number of his officers, switched sides. Thus, the Separatists quickly secured Pavlopil, a village on the eastern bank of the Kalmius River, along with a crossing point. Supported by the 150th Motor Rifle Division, which – despite suffering heavy losses in vehicles and personnel of the 103rd Motor Rifle and the 163rd Tank regiments – secured Vodiane and Chernenko, they took the town of Shyrokyne (a scene of intensive fighting in 2016), and reached Sartana, a small town in the north-eastern suburbs of Mariupol. With the 58th CAA approaching this city from the west, on 28 February the Ministry of Defence in Moscow proudly announced the encirclement of Mairupol – even though this remained incomplete for at least a day longer.

Massive Losses
At this point in time, several events with far-reaching consequences took place. Not only was the mass mobilisation campaign in the DPR suspended, but in the face of stubborn resistance from the ZSU, the Separatist advance slowed down to a creep: Sartana was secured only on 1 March, while a day later they reached the boundaries of the Donetsk Oblast where it meets the coast of the Azov Sea. On Wednesday 2 March, Separatist units – including the Reconnaissance Battalion Sparta and the 100th Motor Rifle Brigade, supported by fighter-bombers of the VKS – fought their way into Volnovakha amid fierce fighting that ruined most of the town. However, in the course of this battle, the VKS lost at least one Su-25, and a helicopter trying to recover its crew. The blockade of Mariupol became firm only on 3 March, by when elements of the DPR's 9th Mariupol-Khingan Motorised Rifle Regiment and troops of the Ministry of Internal Affairs pushed along the coast from Shyrokyne into the eastern districts of Mariupol, and when Pushilin issued a decree incorporating all the villages and towns occupied by that date, and Novoazovsk District, into the DPR para-state for administrative purposes. At this point in time, the DPR deployed another of its units for this attack: the 384th Naval Special Reconnaissance Unit, established in August 2021, probably with the specific purpose of an attack on Mariupol.

Meanwhile, heavy fighting for Volnovakha went on, and the DPR forces there continued suffering heavy losses. On 4 March, the regime in Donetsk reported that its forces had captured seven T-64 MBTs there: however, in turn, it lost the commander of the Sparta Reconnaissance Battalion, Vladimir Zhoga.[8]

Overall, after the first 10 days of the February 2022 Invasion, the territorial gains made by the DPR and LPR were very different. In Luhansk, the LPR managed to cross the Siversky Donets assisted by the VSRF advance in the north, and then to secure most of the Luhansk Oblast by 6 March. By comparison, the DPR had made significant gains in southern Donetsk, helped encircle Mariupol and captured Volnovakha. However, it failed to dislodge the ZSU from several important positions further north: indeed, the DPR forces completely failed to dislodge the Ukrainian armed forces from any of the heavily fortified positions along the LOC between Severodonetsk and Mariinka: not only Sloviansk – the 'spiritual cradle' of the DPR in 2014 – Kramatorsk, and Bakhmut, but also Avdiivka and Kostiantynivka remained firmly under Ukrainian control. Moreover, these gains came at a high price for both the LPR and DPR. Heavily fortified Ukrainian positions and deep minefields constructed along the LOC over the previous eight years exacted a high price from the poorly equipped Separatist forces, which not only lacked modern radios, but even computers and medical kits.

Unsurprisingly, even some of the avidly pro-Russian social media questioned the strategy behind frontal assaults resulting in high casualty rates and slow progress. Reliable statistics are extremely hard to come by, but a Ukrainian investigation based on SBU reporting suggested that the LPR and DPR purposefully obscured the true number of their casualties to prevent panic and demoralisation among their population. According to the same report, in the first two weeks of the offensive, they suffered a combined loss of 3,369, of whom 2,328 were killed and 1,041 wounded. Photographs released in the same report demonstrated that even such figures had been manipulated – allegedly by the Russian FSB – to lessen the number of deaths by a factor 10.[9]

Another principal reason for the extremely high rate of casualties in the Separatist forces – which reached about 10 percent of all their losses from 2014 until 2021 in a matter of two weeks – was the lack of adequate medical care. With losses eventually reaching as much as 55 percent of the original military personnel, the DPR was forced to relaunch the mass conscription suspended on 28 February after only a short hiatus – once Russia's military failure to capture Kyiv and Kharkiv became obvious. Finally, both the mass mobilisation and massive destruction of cities and towns like Mariupol, Volnovakha, and Shchastia, stood in sharp contrast to Putin's stated aim of 'protecting the people of Donbass'.

8
THE RACE TO ODESA

While attracting most public attention, the problems that the Russians and allied Ukrainian Separatists experienced during their advances on Kyiv, Chernihiv, Sumy and Kharkiv were greatly overshadowed by the performance of their two tactical armies deployed to invade southern Ukraine. The 49th CAA, commanded by Lieutenant General Yakov Rezantsev, and the 58th CAA, commanded by an officer of Ukrainian origin: Lieutenant General Mikhail Stepanovich Zusko. Their units managed a near-flawless advance following Putin's original plan. Of course, this came not out of nothing: although too many details remain unclear, there is no doubt that the local terrain and vegetation significantly contributed to this success. Southern Ukraine is a huge and flat plateau, with large distances but – except for the rivers Dnipro and Buh in its west – no major obstacles between the urban centres. Less densely populated than the east and north, cities and towns in this part of the country were also slow to react to the invasion, while the Russians certainly enjoyed support from collaborators in crucial positions within civilian and military authorities of the Kherson and Zaporizhzhya Oblasts. Perhaps of crucial importance: the main ZSU unit protecting this part of Ukraine – the 57th Motorised Brigade, home-based in Nova Kakhova, on the Dnipro River – was 'not at home': it was one of the units defending the LOC, in the Donbass.

Ukrainian against Ukrainians

For yet unexplained reasons, throughout 2014–2022, the ZSU had completely failed to fortify the 'border' with the Russian-occupied Crimean Peninsula, or at least protect road connections between Crimea and the southern Kherson Oblast. Indeed, not one major unit of the Ukrainian armed forces is known to have been deployed in positions opposite the Crimea at the time of the February 2022 invasion.

Arguably, a part of the 35th Naval Infantry Brigade was on an exercise in the Novotroitske area, but without its heavy weapons: these were left behind at that unit's home base in Mykolaiv. In similar fashion, other than Odesa, none of the major cities in this part of the country was protected, and the same was true for the long coasts of the Black and Azov seas. If at all, the ZSU in southern Ukraine was entirely focused on the defence of Mariupol, which as of February 2022 was in the hands of two battalions of the Azov Regiment of the National Guard, one battalion of the 36th Naval Infantry Brigade, and the 12th TD Brigade.

For this set of reasons, the initial Russian advance into southern Kherson and Zaporizhzhya oblasts developed at an extremely high speed: the only reported disturbance to any of the VSRF advances into southern Ukraine during the first hours of invasion may have been the sabotage of the Henichesky Bridge, which was single-handedly blown up by a Marine of the Engineering Battalion of the 35th Naval Infantry Brigade, in which he lost his life.[1] In the east, four amphibious assault ships of the Black Sea Fleet landed a BTG

Table 12: VSRF Forces in southern Ukraine, February–March 2022

Unit	Number of BTGs	Notes
49th Combined Arms Army		OSK South; at least 15 BTG as of 23 February
19th Motorised Rifle Division	3	from 58th CAA, OSK South
20th Guards Motor Rifle Division	6	from 58th CAA, OSK South
177th Naval Infantry Regiment	1 or 2	from the Caspian Sea Flottila, OSK South
810th Guards Naval Infantry Brigade	2	from XXII Army Corps, OSK South
58th Combined Arms Army		from OSK South. 14 BTG as of 23 February
7th Guards Airborne Division	4 to 6	from VDV
42nd Guards Motor Rifle Division	6	from 8th CAA; new division raised in late 2021 by expanding the 20th Motorised Rifle Brigade
136th Guards Motorised Rifle Brigade	2	
336th Guards Naval Infantry Brigade	1	from XI Army Corps, OSK West

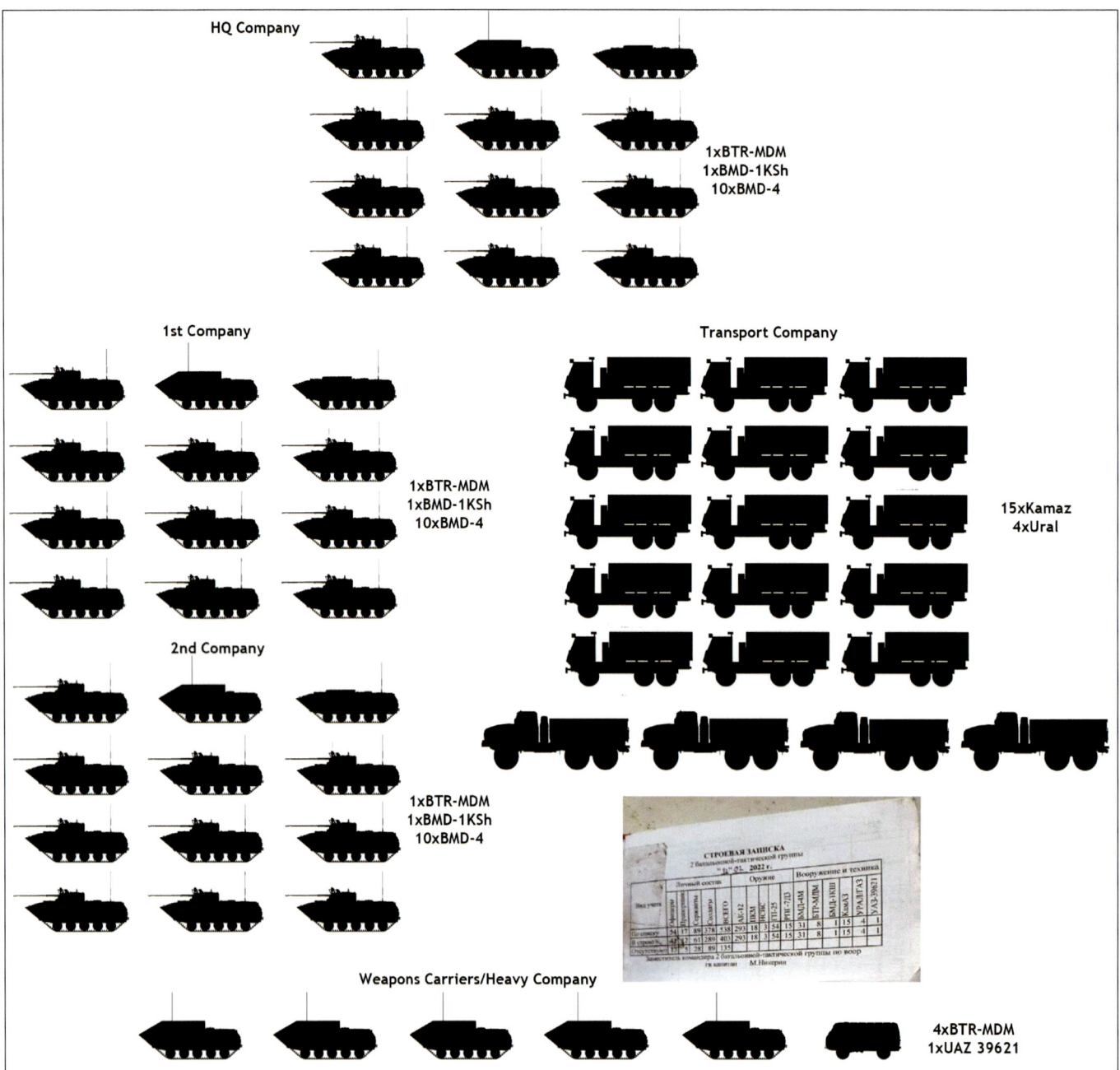

A diagram reconstructing a BTG of the 7th Guards Airborne Division, 58th CAA, based on captured Russian military documentation (inset). As of 22 February 2022, the unit comprised 71 officers, 89 NCOs, and 378 soldiers (for a total of 538 troops), armed with 293 AK-12 assault rifles, 18 PKM and 3 NSVS machine guns, 54 GP-25 grenade launchers and RPG-7DZ rocket propelled grenade launchers, and was mounted on a total of 31 BMD-4Ms, 8 BTR-MDMs, 1 BMD-1KSh, 15 KAMAZ, 4 URALs, and 1 UAZ-39621. (Diagram by Tom Cooper)

of the 810th Naval Infantry Brigade on a beach between Prymorsk and Berdyansk: their appearance took the Ukrainians completely by surprise and remained unopposed, enabling the Russian marines to capture numerous vessels of the Ukrainian Navy (including two Gyurza-class artillery boats, two Zhuk-class patrol boats, a Sorum-class tugboat, and six smaller boats) in the port of Berdyansk, before bringing in their own amphibious assault ships with additional troops, vehicles and supplies. After leaving only a small detachment of military police in the town, on 25 February they launched a rapid advance in the direction of Mariupol, only 70km away.

Fall of Melitopol

Further west, the spearheads of the 42nd Guards Motor Rifle Division made a lightning advance on Melitopol, reaching the outskirts of the town – about 130 kilometres away from their starting point – by the afternoon of 24 February. The appearance of the Russians that deep inside Ukraine certainly shocked many Ukrainians, resulting in a chaos that might have been increased by treason. The 125th Territorial Defence Brigade and the 128th Mountain Assault Brigade were still in the process of being mobilised, and whatever elements were available, were too little and too late: through the evening and the night to 25 February, Zusko's troops surrounded the town, before moving in in the morning, supported by air strikes and artillery. Amid heavy clashes with elements of the 128th, the Russian armour eventually overran the resistance and the civilian leadership surrendered Melitopol in the afternoon of 25 February. A task force of Ukrainian Border Guards that was preparing to launch a counterattack was demolished by attack helicopters and Su-25s of the VKS north of the city, and thus this critical junction of multiple highways and a major railway station was, essentially, under Russian control by the morning of the 26th.

Zusko then not only hurried to deploy his headquarters and establish his main forward supply bases in Melitopol, but now ordered his units to fan out and continue the advance at the highest possible speed. By the end of 25 February, one of his BTGs was on the approaches to Bilozerka and Tokmak, only 80km south of Zaporizhzhya (city); other units were moving in an eastern direction, to meet the 810th Naval Infantry Brigade's advance from the Beredyansk area towards the north. Finally, another BTG of the Naval Infantry rushed all the way to Enerhodar on the Dnipro River, and the nearby Zaporizhzhya Nuclear Power Plant – the biggest of its kind in Europe – before encountering resistance in the form of protesting civilians. After spending the next three days encircling the town and the nuclear power plant, the Russians entered Enerhodar, quickly overpowering resistance from a small group of Territorial Defence troops on 3 March, and secured the giant complex. By then, the spearheads of the 42nd Guards Division had encircled Tokmak – only temporarily slowed down by a counterattack of the 128th on 28 February – and then reached Orehov, south of Zaporizhzhya City: indeed,

A burning Ukrainian T-64 on the streets of Melitopol in late afternoon of 24 February. (Ukrainian Internet)

It was only around 7–8 March 2022, that the 128th Mountain Assault Brigade, ZSU, received its first consignment of Javelin ATGMs. These were promptly put to good use in the Hulaipole area. (Ukrainian MOD)

even as of the morning of 1 March, it appeared as if the Russians might overrun the entire Zaporizhzhya Oblast in a matter of a few days.

What came in between was the 128th Mountain Assault Brigade: the unit had been withdrawn to the Polohy area, but offered bitter resistance to the advance of the 58th CAA. Constantly manoeuvring, it fought one meeting engagement against advancing Russians after the other, until Zusko deployed reinforcements around both of its flanks. To avoid being surrounded, the 128th abandoned its positions and hurriedly withdrew back to the Hulajpole area, where it – finally – managed to establish the ZSU's first firm sector of the frontline in this part of Ukraine, between 7 and 10 March, 2022. Unknown to everybody involved was that in this way the Russian advance on Zaporizhzhya was, finally, checked.

The Race to Dnipro
Early in the morning of 24 February, a combination of heliborne assault by the 7th Guards Airborne Assault Division, 49th CAA, followed by a rapid advance of motorised forces, secured not only the strategically important town of Nova Kakhovka on the Dnipro River, but also the nearby dam and the Kakhovka Hydroelectric Power Plant, with the entry to the North Crimean Canal: the principal sweet water source for Crimea. By all that is known as the time this book was written, this was – by far – the biggest success of the VSRF on the first day of the war. By the afternoon, the airborne assault troops of the 7th Guards were already reinforced by the first of two BTGs of the 126th Coastal Defence Brigade, which advanced over 100 kilometres from their starting point in Armiansk along the T2202 Road within fewer than 12 hours. The Russian spearhead then crossed the Dnipro and established a bridgehead on the western side.

Further west, spearheads of the 20th Motor Rifle Division advancing along the Highway E97, reached Pishchanivka by the late afternoon: only a few kilometres short of Dnipro and 120km from Armiansk. Attack helicopters of the VKS roaming in front of advancing columns caught a retreating ZSU unit and knocked out dozens of its trucks and other vehicles in the Oleshky area. It was only at the approaches to Pishchanivka that the Russians experienced their first clash with the Ukrainians, when part of a column of MT-LB APCs protected by a battery of Tor M1 SAMs

One of the Russian BMP-3 IFVs knocked out by the 128th Mountain Assault Brigade during the fighting on approaches to Hulaipole, between 7 and 10 March 2022. (Ukrainian MOD)

(ASCC/NATO-codename 'SA-15 Gauntlet') was savaged in an attack by Ukrainian Mi-24 helicopter gunships. Nevertheless, by the evening, the Russian troops were on the southern end of the 10-kilometre-long Antonovsky Road Bridge. Following a short clash with about a company of Ukrainian T-64s, and a reconnaissance element mounted on BRDM-2 armoured scout cars, by the next morning the Russians had established their second bridgehead on the western side of the Dnipro, in the Antonivka area.

Fall of Kherson

During the night from 24 to 25 February, Ukrainians hurriedly withdrew whatever units they could from the southern Kherson Oblast. This included most of the S-300s and Buk M1s of the 208th Air Defence Brigade. Early the following morning, a series of sharp clashes took place in the triangle marked by Nova Kakhovka – Radensk – Antonovsky Road Bridge, as several columns of withdrawing Ukrainians became entangled with several columns of advancing Russians. One ZSU unit was hit by the VKS while approaching Radensk, on the E97 highway, losing dozens of vehicles. Nearby, units of the 49th CAA then rapidly secured a major military base together with a huge quantity of ammunition and hundreds of vehicles of all types, from T-64 MBTs, through BMP-1 and BMP-2 IFVs and BTR-60 APCs, to BRDM-2 armoured scout cars and BM-27 multiple rocket launchers. Only hours later, spearheads of the 7th Airborne Division were already in the process of approaching Kherson. Behind them, a group of Ukrainian T-64s, supported by Su-25s of the PSU, took the Russians at the Antonovsky Bridge by surprise: after demolishing a column of enemy artillery approaching from the south, it scattered a company of BMP-2 mounted infantry and destroyed two T-72B3s, but in turn lost four of their own tanks and several BRDMs in the Molodizhne area.

Meanwhile, early that morning, the Russians encircled and – following an artillery barrage – secured Nova Kakhovka, in turn establishing a firm connection to their bridgehead. Immediately after, Rezancev ordered his airborne troops to swing south and rush from Nova Kakhovka down the M14 highway, while pushing additional BTGs from the south-east towards Radensk and Oleshky.

Early on 26 February, the first Russian units approached the Molodizhne area, north-east of Kherson, from two directions. To the Ukrainians, it appeared as if they would quickly withdraw after a short clash with the defenders and several air strikes by the PSU: actually, the Russian airborne troops rerouted their advance to the M14 highway and launched an all-out push on Mykolaiv, followed

A knocked-out MT-LB armoured personnel carrier carrying an anti-aircraft gun mounted on its deck, and a burned-out Tor M1 vehicle of the 20th Guards Motor Rifle Division, seen on the approach to Pishchanivka, late in the afternoon of 24 February. (Ukrainian MOD)

A BMD-1KSh command vehicle and a BMP-2 infantry fighting vehicle seen near the south-eastern end of the Antonovsky Bridge on 25 February 2022. (Ukrainian Internet)

The prime mover of a Russian MSTA-B towed howitzer seen after being knocked out in a Ukrainian ambush outside Radensk. (Ukrainian Internet)

by a column including at least 12 T-72s of the 20th Guards Motor Rifle Division. Rezancev's troops then hardly made any stops: by early 27 February, the spearheads of his 49th CAA briefly probed the defences of Voskresenske and eastern Mykolaiv, before fanning out along the H11, H14, and P06 in a northern direction. Inside Mykolaiv, the 35th Naval Infantry Brigade, reinforced by the balance of the 36th Naval Infantry Brigade, elements of the 59th Motor Infantry Brigade, and the 123rd Territorial Defence Brigade were still in the process of mobilisation, but by the afternoon they did manage to establish a defence perimeter along the H14. Around the same time, the decision was taken to scuttle the flagship of the Ukrainian Navy, the guided missile frigate *Hetman Sahaidachny*, moored in the port of Mykolaiv, to prevent its possible capture by the Russian forces.

Early on 28 February, the 49th CAA completed the isolation of Kherson through securing Chernobaivka and the local airport, before launching their attack into the western outskirts of the city, around 11.00hrs local time. They were held-up for the rest of the day by slowly growing Ukrainian resistance. After bringing additional elements of the 20th Guards Motor Rifle into position, early on 1 March 2022, the 49th CAA launched its major attack from north and east, supported by a strong artillery barrage: this breached the ZSUs defences and by noon numerous Russian troops and vehicles were deep inside the city. The next day, Kherson surrendered, becoming the first – and only – capital of any Ukrainian oblast captured by the Russians.

A T-64 of the ZSU captured by the Russians in Radensk. (Russian MOD)

Rosgvardia troops protecting the Russian flag they had raised in a square in downtown Kherson in early April 2022. (Rosgvardia release)

Disaster in Voznesensk

The assault on Kherson had not even started when Rezancev received the order to push further west – to Odesa. With the ZSU garrison in Mykolaiv blocking the way along the H14 highway, he needed an alternative route. The solution was found in Voznesensk, a town about 100km north of Mykolaiv: the nearest place with a bridge over the Buh River, and a town with a disused air base nearby.

Travelling minor roads between the H11 and H14 before reaching P06 and turning north, the spearheads of the 126th Coastal Defence Brigade had reached the area on 28 February. However, their movement was reported by the population and ZSU reconnaissance and an alert sounded all the way to Kyiv: seriously concerned about the growing crisis, the GenStab-U reacted by rushing the 80th Airborne Assault Brigade from its base in Lviv to the Mykolaiv Oblast. Arriving in Voznesensk early on 1 March, Ukrainian paratroopers deployed reconnaissance parties down the P55 and P06 highways, to set up ambushes for the approaching Russians. Meanwhile, their commander, Colonel Ihor Skybiuk, deployed the rest of his unit, and the local volunteers into a u-shaped position around the P06 in the southern part of the town: 'The Russian tactics while approaching Voznesensk were effective. They used reconnaissance to avoid our ambush positions. In some cases, we had to retreat to avoid getting encircled.'[2]

All the time monitoring the Russian advance with help of the population and reconnaissance UAVs, Skybiuk and his troops were able to further improve their positions before the enemy attack. Rezancev launched his onslaught early in the morning of 2 March in the form of a two-prong attack: by means of another heliborne attack (this time by the 247th Guards VDV Regiment), and by two assault parties on the ground. Probably launched from the Nova Kakhovka area, the helicopter formation included Mi-8s loaded with airborne troops, escorted by Mi-24s and Mi-35 helicopter gunships. It travelled well to the north before turning north-west, with the intention of reaching Voznesensk. However, underway at

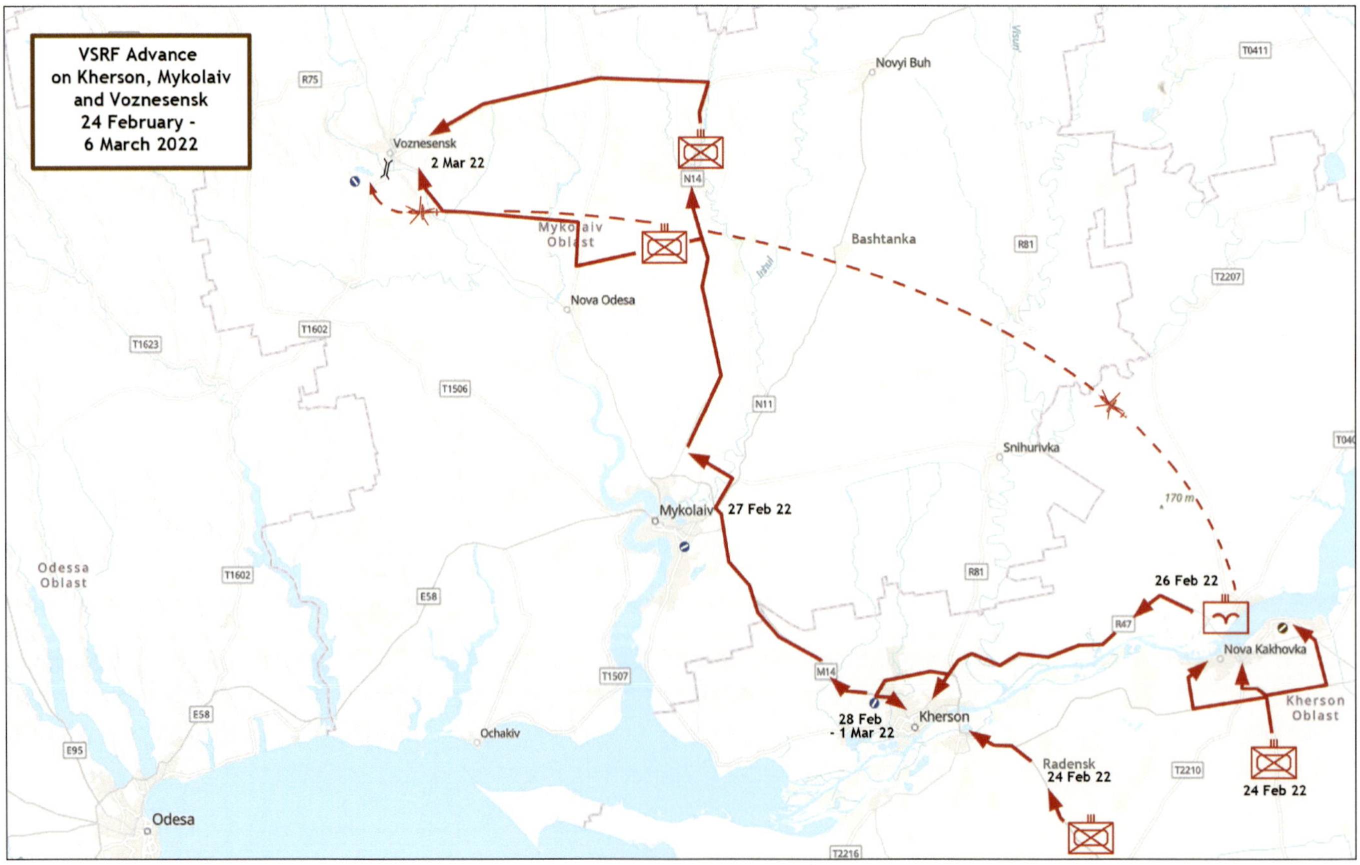

A map of the 49th CAA's advance to Kherson and Nova Kakhova, to Mykolaiv, and the raid on Voznesensk. (Map by Tom Cooper)

WAR IN UKRAINE VOLUME 2: RUSSIAN INVASION, FEBRUARY 2022

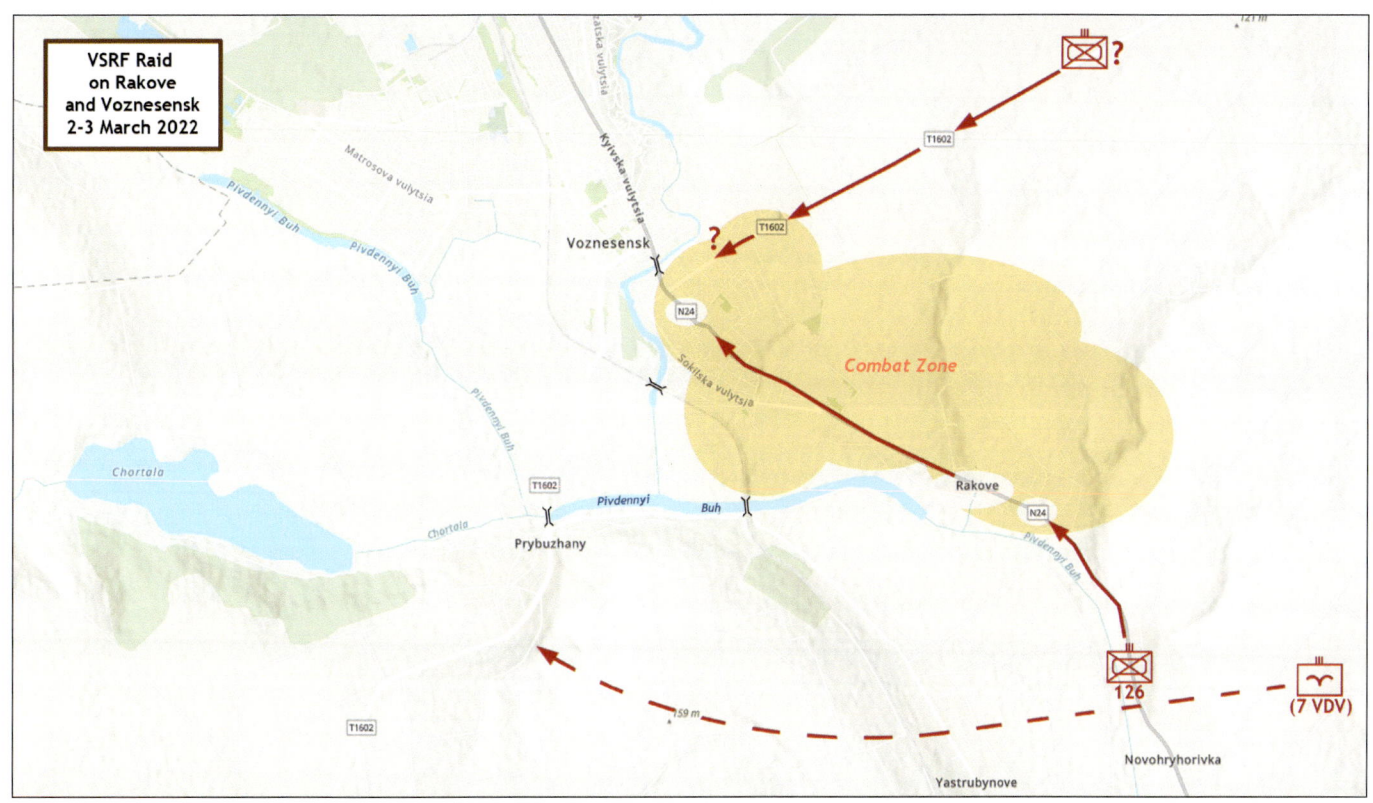

A map of the Russian attack on Voznesensk on 2 March 2022. Notably, while the attack of the 126th Coastal Defence Brigade via Rakove into the southern part of the town, and the heliborne landing 'on a hill south-west of the town' by the 247th Guards VDV Regiment have been cross-confirmed, it remains unclear if the Russians also attempted to attack along the T1602 highway. (Map by Tom Cooper)

A destroyed T-72B3 main battle tank of either the 126th Coastal Defence Brigade or the 20th Guards Motor Rifle Division, seen outside the southern outskirts of Voznesensk. Visible to the rear right is one of the bridges which the Russians aimed to reach. (Ukrainian MOD)

low altitude it ran straight into the positions of the 17th Tank Brigade in the Bashtanka area, where a number of its helicopters and one of the escorting Su-30s were shot down by Ukrainian MANPADs.

Meanwhile, the assault party of the 20th Guards Motor Rifle Division was in the process entering southern Voznesensk when it ran into an ambush: when the column stopped, it was hit by a murderously precise barrage from 80th Airborne's artillery group, and then by multiple anti-tank teams. Behind it, the BTG of the 126th Coastal Defence Brigade pressed its attack home, reached the Bolgarka area of southern Voznesensk and, moving quickly, turned west in the direction of the crucial bridge spanning the Buh River, as Skybiuk explained: 'That's where we had set up our fire pocket in

A scene that occurred hundreds of times all over Ukraine in late February and early March 2022: a Russian APC – in this case a BTR-80 captured during the battle of Voznesensk on 2 March – being towed away by a Ukrainian tractor. (Ukrainian MOD)

The tailfin of a VKS Mi-24 shot down outside Bashtanka on 2 March 2022. (Ukrainian MOD)

Ukrainian troops with a captured BMD-3, outside Mykolaiv, on 2 March 2022. (Ukrainian MOD)

cooperation with the Territorial Defence: a courageous guy blew up the bridge and then we hit them from all sides, knocking out tanks and infantry fighting vehicles.'

The ground attack had barely begun when the survivors of the Russian helicopter formation hit by MANPADS over the Bashtanka area appeared on the scene to disgorge airborne troops on the western bank of the Buh, south-west of Voznesensk. Skybiuk promptly redirected his artillery in that direction, before ordering a counterattack. Shaken by heavy losses, the surviving Russians retreated into the night. Exact figures remain evasive, but in grand total, the Ukrainians in Voznesensk claimed to have shot down one Mi-24 and reported the destruction or capture of between 15 and 17 tanks, and 30 other vehicles, while locals reported the death of at least 100 Russian troops and the capture of 10: there is little doubt that this raid ended in a veritable disaster. The 49th CAA lost not only a BTG of airborne troops, but the best part of a BTG from the 126th Coastal Defence Brigade, including most of its artillery. The Ukrainians did suffer losses of their own, but Voznesensk remained firmly in their hands. Of primary importance however was that the VSRF's drive on Odesa was definitely checked and was never to be resumed, because the 49th CAA suffered such heavy losses that it lost its offensive capability.[3]

Certainly enough, Putin was not ready to give up and thus Rezencev received strict orders to take both Mykolaiv and Voznesensk regardless of the cost. Although critically short of troops, he continued engaging the Ukrainians in the area between Bashtanka, via Katerynivka to Voznesensk for a week longer. Moreover, after receiving reinforcements of airborne troops, early on

Ukrainian soldier inspecting a knocked out BMD-2M of the 108th Airborne Assault Regiment, 7th Airborne Division outside Mykolaiv, first week of March 2022. (Ukrainian MOD)

6 March he launched an attack on Kulbakyne Airport, outside Mykolaiv. Once again, the Ukrainian reaction was as quick as lethal: another BTG of assailants was mauled, with scores of its troops either killed or captured. After these two catastrophes, the writing was on the wall: a task force of the Russian Black Sea Fleet underway off the coast and waiting to bolster the advance on Odesa by an amphibious assault, was recalled to Sevastopol only a day later.

Failure of Plan A

With this, the opening blows of the Russian invasion of Ukraine in 2022 had been delivered, and an all-out war was in full swing. Contrary to all expectations, a combination of massive resistance by the population, the stubbornness of the government in Kyiv, and much more effective operations of the ZSU in the north, north-east, and east than ever expected, effected a quick collapse of what can be described as 'Putin's Plan A': a coup in Kyiv and a quick conquest of about half of Ukraine. Even if the dictator in Moscow might not have wanted to accept this, it was already obvious at that point that his 'special military operation' was an abysmal failure and Russia in no position to win the war. Nevertheless, always bolstered by outright masterpieces of his propaganda machinery, Vladimir Putin remained insistent. Therefore, the war went on and was even intensified over the following months. That story is going to be told in the following volumes of this sub-series.

APPENDICES

I

Known Major Units of the Ukrainian Army, Territorial Defence & National Guard as of February 2022		
Unit	HQ/Garrison	Notes
Directly Subordinated Units		
15th Rocket Artillery Regiment	Drogobych	equipped with BM-30 Smerch MLRS
19th Rocket Artillery Brigade "Saint Barbara"	Khmelnytskyi	four divisions with a total of 12 9K79-1 Tochka-U TEL; 7th Motorised Infantry Battalion attached
107th Rocket Artillery Regiment	Kremenchuk	four divisions of BM-30 Smerch MLRS; reassigned to OK North in February 2022, then to OK East in March or April 2022
27th Rocket Artillery Brigade "Sumy"	Sumy	four divisions of BM-27 Uragan MLRS reassigned to OK North in February2022
43rd Artillery Brigade "Hetman Taras Tryasyl"	Divychki	established 2014; four divisions of 2S7 Pion; reassigned to OK North in February 2022; 45th Motor Infantry Battalion attached
Airborne Assault Command		
25th Airborne Brigade "Sicheslavska"	Hvardiiske	equipped with BMD-1, BMD-2 and BTR-4; reassigned to OK East in February 2022
45th Air Assault Brigade	Belhorod	established 2016; equipped with BTR-3; reassigned to OK South in February 2022
46th Air Assault Brigade	Poltava	established 2016; reassigned to the OK North, February 2022
81st Air Assault Brigade	Druzhykivka	established 2014; including 87th Airborne Assault Battalion; reassigned to the OK East, February 2022
79th Air Assault Brigade	Mykolaiv	established 2007; reassigned to the OK South, February 2022
95th Air Assault Brigade	Zhytomir	including 13th Airborne Assault Battalion; partially equipped with BTR-4; reassigned to the OK North, February 2022
OK North (HQ Chernihiv) CO of January 2022: Major General Victor Nikolyuk		
16th OBrAA	Brody	Mi-24P/PU1, Mi-8MT/MTV/MSB-V
1139th Anti-Aircraft Missile Regiment	Bila Tserkva	5 battalions with Osa-AKM
1st Operational Brigade NG	Vyshhorod	acting presidential guard, three infantry battalions, a battalion each of tank, artillery and anti-aircraft artillery
4th Rapid Reaction Brigade NG	Hostomel	two infantry battalions, a battalion each of tank (T-64BV), artillery and anti-aircraft defence; UAV detachment
1st Tank Brigade "Severia"	Honcharivske	established 1997; 1st, 2nd, and 3rd Tank Battalions with T-64BV; 4th Mech Battalion with BMP-2; CO as of 24 February 22: Colonel Ihor Shpak
26th Artillery Brigade	Berdychiv	pre-2014 unit; 1st and 2nd Divisions with 2S19, 3rd Division with 2S5, 4th (AT) with MT-12, 14th Motorised Infantry Battalion
30th Mechanised Brigade "Prince Konstantyn Ostrogski"	Novohrad-Volynskyi	established 1992; 1st, 2nd, 3rd, Tank Battalions with T-64B/BV; 2nd Motorised Infantry Battalion attached
58th Motorised Infantry Brigade	Sumy	established 2015; 13th, 14th and 15th Motorised Infantry Battalions; tank company equipped with T-72AV or T-72B1
72nd Mechanised Brigade "Chornykh Zaporozhtsiv"	Bila Tserkva	established 1992; T-64B/BV; 12th Motorised Infantry Battalion attached
1129th Anti-Aircraft Missile Regiment	Bila Tserkva	five batteries with Osa-AKM
61st Jaeger Brigade	Zhytomir	established 2015
112th Brigade TD	Kyiv	
114th Brigade TD	Brovary	
115th Brigade TD	Zhytomyr	

Known Major Units of the Ukrainian Army, Territorial Defence and National Guard as of February 2022 (continued)

116th Brigade TD	Poltava	
117th Brigade TD	Sumy	
118th Brigade TD	Cherkasy	
119th Brigade TD	Chernihiv	
OK East (HQ Dnipro)		
18th OBrAA	Poltava	Mi-24P/PU1, Mi-8MT/MTV/MSB-V, Mi-2MSB-2
3rd Operational Brigade, National Guard	Kharkiv	including three infantry battalions (each with tank, artillery and anti-aircraft artillery companies)
17th Tank Brigade "Konstantin Pestushko"	Dnipro	established 1992. 1st, 2nd, and 3rd Tank Battalions (T-64B and BV), Mechanised Battalion with BMP-1. 40th Motorised Infantry Battalion attached
35th Naval Infantry Brigade	Dachne	including 18th and 137th Naval Infantry Battalions
53rd Mechanised Brigade "Prince Vladimir Monomakh"	Severodonetsk	established 2014; two mechanised battalions, 24th and 43rd Motorised Infantry Battalions; tank battalion with T-72AV/B & T-64BV
54th Mechanised Brigade	Bakhmut	established 2014. 25th and 46th Motorised Infantry Battalions attached
55th Artillery Brigade "Zaporozhian Sich"	Zaporizhia	three divisions with 12 2A65 each; 39th Motor Infantry Battalion attached
92nd Mechanised Brigade "Ivan Sirko"	Bashkirivka	two mechanised battalions only, partially equipped with BTR-4; 22nd Motor Infantry Battalions, two tank battalions with T-64BV
93rd Mechanised Brigade "Kholodny Yar"	Cherkaske	20nd Motorised Infantry Battalion attached
1039th Anti-Aircraft Missile Regiment	Hvardiiske	equipped with Osa-AKM
108th Brigade TD	Dnipro	
109th Brigade TD	Mariupol	
110th Brigade of TD	Zaporizhia	
111th Brigade TD	Severodonetsk	
113th Brigade TD	Kharkiv	
OK South (HQ Odesa)		
11th OBrAA	Kherson	Mi-24P/PU1, Mi-8MT/MTV/MSB-V
38th Anti-Aircraft Missile Regiment	Chornomorske	five batteries Osa-AKM
18th Special Operation Regiment Azov (NG)	Mariupol	two infantry battalions, one tank company (T-64BM), one artillery battalion (D-30 and 120mm mortars); CO as of 19 March: Major Denys Prokopenko
28th Mechanised Brigade	Chornomorske	established 1992; tank battalion equipped with T-64BV, mechanised battalions with BMP-1, BMP-2 and BTR-80; 18th Motorised Infantry Battalion attached
32nd Naval Rocket Artillery Brigade	Altestove	one division with BM-27 Uragan, two divisions with BM-21 Grad
36th Naval Infantry Brigade "Rear Admiral Mikhail Bilinsky"	Mykolaiv	including 501st and 503rd Naval Infantry Battalions, tank battalion with T-64. CO in Mid-March 2022: Colonel Volodomyr Beranyuk
56th Motorised Infantry Brigade	Mariupol	established 2015: 21st, 23rd and 37th Motorised Infantry Battalions; tank company equipped with T-72AV or B1
57th Motorised Infantry Brigade "Kostya Gordienko"	Kropyvnytskyi	established 2014; 17th, 34th and 42nd Motorised Infantry Battalions; tank company equipped with T-72AV or B1
59th Motorised Infantry Brigade "Yakov Gandziuk"	Haisyn	established 2014; 9th, 10th and 11th Motorised Infantry Battalions; tank company equipped with T-72AV or B1
40th Artillery Brigade "Grand Duke Vytautas"	Pervomaisk	established 2015; 1st and 2nd Division with 2A36 Giatsint-B, 3rd and 4th with 2A65 Msta-B, 19th Motorised Infantry Battalion attached
38th Anti-Aircraft Missile Regiment	Chornomorske	five batteries with OSA-AKM systems
120th Brigade TD	Vinnytsia	
121st Brigade TD	Kropyvnytskyi	
122nd Brigade TD	Odesa	

Known Major Units of the Ukrainian Army, Territorial Defence and National Guard as of February 2022 *(continued)*		
123rd Brigade TD	Mykolaiv	
124th Brigade TD	Kherson	
OK West (HQ Rivne)		
12th OBrAA	Novi Kalnyiv	Mi-24P/PU1, Mi-8MT/MTV/MSB-V
39th Anti-Aircraft Missile Regiment	Volodymyr-Volynksyi	four battalions Osa-AKM
10th Naval Aviation Brigade	Mykolaiv	10 Mi-8MSB-V, Ka-27, Ka-226, Mi-14, 2 An-2, 6 TB.2
10th Mountain Assault Brigade	Kolomyia	established October 2015. 1st, 108th, 109th Mountain Assault Battalions, partly equipped with BMP-1 and -2; 8th Motorised Infantry Battalion attached; tank battalion equipped with 31 T-72AV and T-72B1
128th Mountain Assault Brigade "Zakarpattia"	Mukacheve	pre-2014 unit; 15th Mountain Assault Battalion, 21st and 36th Mechanised Battalions, 16th Tank Battalion equipped with 31 T-72AV and T-72B1
14th Mechanised Brigade "Prince Roman the Great"	Volodymyr-Volynskyi	established December 2014; 1st Motorised Infantry Battalion attached; tank battalion equipped with T-64BV and a batch of six T-84
24th Mechanised Brigade "King Daniel of Galicia"	Yavoriv	established 2003; 3rd Motorised Infantry Battalion attached; tank battalion equipped with T-72AV
44th Artillery Brigade	Ternopil	Formed September 2014. 1st Division equipped with 2A65 Msta-B, 2nd and 3rd Divisions with 2A36 Giatsint-B and 4th Division with 2S7 Pion. 6th Motorised Infantry Battalion attached
39th Anti-Aircraft Missile Regiment	Volodymyr-Volynskyi	Equipped with OSA-K (SA-8b)
80th Air Assault Brigade	Lviv	pre-2014 unit; administrated by the DshV Command
100th Brigade TD	Lutsk	
101st Brigade TD	Uzhhorod	
102nd Brigade TD	Ivano-Frankivsk	
103rd Brigade TD	Lviv	
104th Brigade TD	Rivne	
105th Brigade TD	Ternopil	
106th Brigade TD	Khmelnytskyi	
107th Brigade TD	Chernivtsi	
2nd Operational Brigade, National Guard	Lviv	four infantry battalions
Reserve Corps		
3rd Tank Brigade	Yarmolyntsi	established 2016 as a reserve (cadre) unit; tank battalions equipped with T-72, mechanised battalion with BMP-1; possibly converted to a regular unit in 2019 and assigned to OK North
4th Tank Brigade	N/A	established 2017 as a reserve (cadre) unit. Tank battalions equipped with T-64 Bulat and BV, mechanised battalion with BMP-1
5th Tank Brigade	N/A	established 2016 as a reserve (cadre) unit. Tank battalions equipped with T-72, mechanised battalion with BMP-1
60th Mechanised Brigade	N/A	
62rd Mechanised Brigade	N/A	established 2016–2017
63h Mechanised Brigade	N/A	established 2016–2017
66th Mechanised Brigade	N/A	
38th Artillery Brigade	N/A	
45th Artillery Brigade	N/A	towed artillery

II

Primary Combat Units of the SV/VSRF, 2014	
Unit	Notes
OSK West (HQ Saint Petersburg)	
45th Artillery Brigade	2S4 Tulipan and 2S7 Psion
79th Guards Rocket Artillery Brigade	9K515 Tornado-S 300mm MLRS
112th Missile Brigade	9K720 Iskander ballistic missiles
Operational Group of Russian Forces in Transnistria	82nd and 113th Motorised Rifle Battalions
1st Guards Tank Army	**HQ Odintsovo**
2nd Guards Motorised Rifle Division "Tamanskaya"	1st and 15th Motorised Rifle, 1st Tank and 147th Artillery regiments. Equipped with T-72B3 and T-90A
4th Guards Tank Division "Kantemirovskaya"	12 and 13th Tank, 423rd Motorised Rifle and 275th Artillery regiments. Equipped with T-80U, UE-1, BVM and BV
6th Independent Tank Brigade	Equipped with T-72B3
27th Motorised Rifle Brigade	Tank battalion equipped with T-90A and T-90M
6th Combined Arms Army	**HQ Saint Petersburg**
25th Guards Motorised Rifle Brigade	
138th Guards Motorised Rifle Brigade	Tank battalion equipped with T-72B3 and T-80BV
9th Guards Artillery Brigade	2S19 SPG
26th Missile Brigade	9K720 Iskander ballistic missiles
20th Guards Combined Arms Army	HQ Voronezh
3rd Motorised Rifle Division	252nd and 752nd Motorised Rifle, 237th Tank and 99th Artillery regiments. Equipped with T-72B and B3
144th Motorised Rifle Division	254th and 488th Motorised Rifle, 59th Tank and 856th Artillery regiments. Equipped with T-72B and BA
236th Artillery Brigade	
448th Missile Brigade	Iskander ballistic missiles
11th Army Corps	**HQ Kaliningrad**
18th Motorised Rifle Division	79th, 275th and 280th Motorised Rifle and 11th Tank regiments. Equipped with T-72B3 tanks
152nd Missile Brigade	Iskander ballistic missiles
244th Artillery Brigade	BM-27 Uragan and BM-30 Smerch MLRS
336th Guards Naval Infantry Brigade	Two battalions with BTR-82, one airborne battalion
OSK South (HQ Rostov-On-Don)	
102nd Military Base	Gyumri, Armenia
439th Guards Rocket Artillery Brigade	BM-27 Uragan and BM-30 Smerch MLRS
8th Combined Arms Army	**HQ Novotcherkassk**
20th Motorised Rifle Division	Formed at the end of 2021 from the 20th Motorised Infantry Brigade. At least one Tank battalion equipped with T-72B3
150th Motorised Rifle Division	102nd and 103rd Motorised Rifle, 68th and 163rd Tank and 381st Artillery regiments. Equipped with T-72B and B3
47th Missile Brigade	Iskander
238th Artillery Brigade	2A65 guns and BM-27 Uragan MRLS
22nd Army Corps	HQ Simferopol
126th Coastal Defence Brigade	Akin to a Motorised Rifle Brigade
810th Naval Infantry Brigade	
15th Rocket Artillery Brigade	

Primary Combat Units of the SV/VSRF, 2014 *(continued)*	
49th Combined Arms Army	**HQ Stavropol**
7th Military Base	Gudauta (Abkhazia), akin to a Motorised Rifle Brigade, includes a Tank Battalion with T-72B3
34th Motorised Rifle Brigade	
205th Motorised Rifle Brigade	Tank battalion equipped with T-72B3
1st Guards Missile Brigade	Iskander ballistic missiles
227th Artillery Brigade	Two SPG and one MLRS battalions
58th Combined Arms Army	**HQ Vladikavkaz**
4th Military Base	Tskhinvali (South Ossetia). Akin to a Motorised Rifle Brigade
19th Motorised Rifle Division	429th and 503rd Motorised Rifle regiments. One T-90A equipped Tank Battalion
42nd Motorised Rifle Division	70th, 71st, 291st Motorised Rifle and 50th Artillery regiments. Equipped with T-72B3
136th Guards Motorised Rifle Brigade	Tank battalion equipped with 40 T-90A
12th Missile Brigade	Iskander ballistic missiles
OSK Centre	
90th Tank Division	6th, 80th and 239th Tank, 228th Motorised Rifle and 400th Artillery regiments. T-72A, AB, B, and B3 tanks
232nd Rocket Artillery Brigade	Two divisions with 16 BM-27 Uragan
2nd Guards Combined Arms Army	**HQ Samara**
15th Guards Motorised Rifle Brigade	
21st Guards Motorised Rifle Brigade	Two tank battalions with 40 T-72BA and 40 T-72B3
30th Motorised Rifle Brigade	
92nd Missile brigade	Iskander ballistic missiles
385th Guards Artillery Brigade	
41st Combined Arms Army	**HQ Novossibirsk**
35th Guards Motorised Rifle Brigade	Tank battalion equipped with T-72B
55th Motorised Rifle Brigade	
74th Guards Motorised Rifle Brigade	Tank battalion equipped with T-72B3
201st Military Base	Dushanbe (Tadjikistan). Akin to a Motorised Rifle Division. 149th, 92nd and 191st Motorised Rifle Regiments. Separate Tank Battalion
119th Missile brigade	Iskander ballistic missiles
120th Guards Artillery Brigade	
OSK East (HQ Khabarovsk)	
5th Combined Arms Army	**HQ Oussouriisk**
127th Motorised Rifle Division	114th and 394th Motorised Rifle and 218th Tank regiments. Equipped with T-72B
57th Guards Motorised Rifle Brigade	Tank battalion equipped with T-80BV
60th Motorised Rifle Brigade	Tank battalion equipped with T-72B
20th Guards Missile Brigade	Iskander missiles
305th Artillery Brigade	
29th Combined Arms Army	HQ Tchita
36th Guards Motorised Rifle Brigade	Tank battalion equipped with 31 T-72B3
3rd Missile Brigade	Iskander ballistic missiles
200th Artillery Brigade	
35th Combined Arms Army	**HQ Belogorsk**
38th Guards Motorised Rifle Brigade	Tank battalion equipped with T-80BV
64th Motorised Rifle Brigade	Tank battalion equipped with T-80BV and BVM
69th Covering Brigade	Akin to Motorised Rifle Brigade. Tank battalion equipped with T-80BV
107th Missile Brigade	Iskander missiles

Primary Combat Units of the SV/VSRF, 2014 *(continued)*	
165th Artillery Brigade	
36th Combined Arms Army	**HQ Oulan-Oude**
5th Guards Tank Brigade	Equipped with T-72B
37th Guards Motorised Rifle Brigade	Tank battalion equipped with T-72B3
30th Artillery Brigade	
103rd Missile Brigade	Iskander missiles
68th Army Corps	
18th Machine Gun and Artillery Division	46th and 49th Infantry Regiments. Two Separate Tank Companies with T-72B
39th Motorised Infantry Brigade	Tank battalion equipped with T-80BV
Pacific Fleet	**Vladivostock**
155th Guards Naval Infantry Brigade	Separate Tank Company with 10 T-80BV
40th Naval Infantry Brigade	Separate Tank Company with 10 T-80BV
520th Rocket Artillery Brigade	
Northern Fleet and Joint Arctic OSK	
14th Corps	
61st Naval Infantry Brigade	
80th Motorised Rifle Brigade	
200th Independent Motorised Rifle Brigade	Tank battalion equipped with T-80BVM

III

VKS and VMF, Major Units, 2018-2022[1]		
DA: Long-range Aviation (HQ Moscow)		
203rd OAP SZ	Dyagilevo	Il-78
22nd Heavy Bomber Aviation Division (TBAD)	Engels	
121st TBAP	Engels	One squadron each of Tu-160 and Tu-95MS
52nd TBAP	Shaykovka	Two squadrons of Tu-22M3
40th SAP	Vysokiy	One squadron of Tu-22M3
326th TBAD	HQ Ukrainka	
182nd TBAP	Ukrainka	Three squadrons of Tu-95MS
200th TBAP	Belaya	Two squadrons of Tu-22M3
VTA: Military Transport Aviation (HQ Moscow)		
12th Military Transport Aviation Division (VTAD)	Engels	
196th VTAP	Migalovo	Two squadrons Il-76, several An-22
334th VTAP	Kresty	Two squadrons Il-76
556th VTAP	Seshcha	One squadron each of An-124 and Il-76
18th VTAD	Orenburg	
117th VTAP	Orenburg	One squadron with An-12PPS and Il-22PP, one with An-2, 26 and 72, two squadrons with Il-76
235th VTAP	Ulyanovsk	One squadron each of An-2 and Il-76, several An-124
708th VTAP	Taganrog	Two squadrons of Il-76
610th TsBP PLS	Ivanovo Severnyi	One squadron each of A-50, An-2 and Il-76
4th Air and Air Defence Army (attached to OSK South, HQ Rostov-on-Don)		
30th OTSAP	Rostov-on-Don	N/A transport aircraft
3624th Aviation Base (AvB)	Erebuni (Armenia)	One squadron of Su-30SM, one composite squadron of helicopters
16th Army Aviation Brigade (Br AA)	Zernograd	Two squadrons of Mi-8 and two of Mi-28N and Mi-35M, detachment of Mi-26

VKS and VMF, Major Units, 2018-2022[1] *(continued)*		
55th OVP	Korenovsk	One squadron of Mi-8, one of Mi-28N and Mi-35M, and one of Ka-52
487th OVP	Budyonnovsk	One squadron with Mi-8, two squadrons with Mi-24, Mi-28N and Mi-35M, one squadron with Forpost UAV
31st Air Defence Division	Crimea	Two regiments, S-300PM, S-400, Pantsir-S
51st Air Defence Division	Novocherkassk	Three regiments, Buk, S-300PM, S-400, Pantsir-S
1st Composite Aviation Division (SAD)	Krymsk	
3rd SAP	Krymsk	Two squadrons with Su-27M3 and Su-30M2, one squadron of Su-27
31st IAP	Millerovo	Two squadrons of Su-30SM
559th BAP	Morozovsk	Three squadrons of Su-34
4th SAD	Marinovka	
11th SAP	Marinovka	Two squadrons of Su-24M, one of Su-24MR
368th ShAP	Budyonnovsk	Two squadrons of Su-25SM and SM3
960th ShAP	Primorsko-Akhtarsk	Two squadrons of Su-25SM and SM3
27th SAD	Belbek	
37th SAP	Gvardeyskoye	One squadron each of Su-24M and Su-25SM
38th IAP	Belbek	Two squadrons of Su-27
39th VP	Dzhankoy	One squadron each of Ka-52 and Mi-8 a third with Mi-28N and Mi-35M
Naval Aviation of the Black Sea Fleet (attached to the OSK South, HQ Sevastopol)		
43rd OMShAP	Saki	One squadron Su-24M, MR, one squadron with Su-30SM
318th OSAP	Kacha	One squadron with An-26 and Mi-8, one with Ka-27 and 29, detachments of Be-12 and Forpost UAV
6th Air Force and Air Defence Army (attached to OSK West, HQ Saint Petersburg)		
15th Br AA	Ostrov	One Squadron each of Ka-52 and Mi-8, one squadron of Mi-28N and Mi-35M, one detachment of Mi-26
33rd OTSAP	Levashovo	An-26, An-72, An-148, Tu-134, Mi-8
332nd OVP	Pushkin	One squadron of Mi-8, two squadrons with Mi-28N, Mi-35M and Mi-24
440th OVP	Vyazma	One squadron of Ka-52, two squadrons with Mi-8
2nd Air Defence Division	Saint Petersburg	Five regiments. Buk, S-300PS, S-300V S-400, Pantsir-S
32nd Air Defence Division	Tver	Two regiments. S-300PS and S-300PM
105th SAD	Voronezh	
14th IAP	Khalino	Two squadrons Su-30SM, one squadron MiG-29SMT
47th SAP	Buturlinovka	Two squadrons of Su-34
159th IAP	Besovets	Two squadrons of Su-35S, one squadron of Su-27SM
790th IAP	Khotilovo	Two squadrons MiG-31BM and one squadron of Su-35S
Naval Aviation of the Baltic Sea Fleet (attached to the OSK West, HQ Kaliningrad)		
4th MshAP	Chkalovsk	One squadron each of Su-24M and Su-30SM. One Forpost UAV detachment
689th IAP	Chkalovsk	Two squadrons of Su-27
11th Air Force and Air Defence Army (attached to OSK East, HQ Khabarovsk)		
18th Br AA	Khabarovsk Tsentralnyi	One squadron each of Mi-8, Ka-52 and one with Mi-26 and Mi-8
35th OTSAP	Khabarovsk Tsentralnyi	An-12, An-26, Tu-134 and Tu-154
120th OIAP	Domna	Two Su-30SM squadrons
112th OVP	Chita Cheryomushki	Two squadrons of Mi-8 and one of Mi-24P

VKS and VMF, Major Units, 2018-2022[1] (continued)		
266th OShAP	Domna	Two Su-25 squadrons, one UAV squadron
319th OVP	Chernigovka	One squadron each of Mi-8 and Ka-52, detachment of Mi-26
25th Air Defence Division	Komsomolsk-on-Amur	Three regiments, S-300PS, S-300PM, S-300V
26th Air Defence Division	Chita	One regiment, S-300PS
93rd Air Defence Division	Vladivostok	Two regiments, S-300V, S-400, Pantsir-S
303rd SAD	Khurba	
18th ShAP	Chernigovka	Two squadrons with Su-25SM
22nd IAP	Tsentralnaya Uglovaya	Two squadrons with MiG-31BM and one with Su-35S
23rd IAP	Dzyomgi	Two Su-35S squadrons
277th BAP	Khurba	Two squadrons with Su-34 and one with Su-24M2
Naval Aviation of the Pacific Fleet (attached to the OSK East, HQ Vladivostok)		
317th OSAP	Yelizovo	One squadron with Il-38 and Il-38N, one squadron with Ka-27, one squadron with MiG-31BM, one UAV squadron with Forpost and Orlan-10, An-12 and An-26 detachment
7062th Aviation Base	Nikolayevka	One Anti-Submarine Warfare, and one Transport squadron
14th Air Force and Air Defence Army (attached to OSK Centre, HQ Yekaterinburg)		
17th Br AA	Kamensk Uralsky	One squadron each of Mi-8 and Mi-24P, one squadron with Mi-8 and Mi-26
32nd OTSAP	Koltsovo	An-12, An-26, An-148 and Mi-8
337th OVP	Tolmachovo	One squadron each with Mi-24P and Mi-8
41st Air Defence Division	Ob	Three regiments with S-300PM, S-300PS and S-400
76th Air Defence Division	Samara	Three regiments with S-300PS
21st SAD	Chelyabinsk	
2nd SAP	Shagol	One squadron of Su-24MR, two squadrons of Su-34
712th IAP	Kansk	Two squadrons of MiG-31BM
764th IAP	Bolshoye Savino	Two squadrons of MiG-31BM
45th Air Force and Air Defence Army (attached to Northern Fleet and Joint Arctic OSK, HQ Severomorsk)		
98th OSAP	Monchegorsk	One squadron each of Su-24M, Su-24MR and MiG-31BM
7050th Aviation Base	Severomorsk	One squadron each of Il-38N and Ka-27, one with Ka-27PS, Ka-29 and Mi-8, a fourth with An-12, Il-18 and Tu-134, a fight, independent, with Tu-142MK and Tu-142MR
1st Air Defence Division	Severomorsk	Four regiments with S-300, S-400 and Pantsir-S
Shipborne Aviation Division	Severomorsk	
100th KIAP	Severomorsk	MiG-29KR/KUBR
279th KIAP	Severomorsk	Two squadrons of Su-33, one of Su-25UTG

BIBLIOGRAPHY

Beehner, L., *Analyzing the Russian Way of War; Evidence from the 2008 Conflict with Georgia* (West Point: Modern War Institute, 2018)

Butowski, P., *Flashpoint Russia; Russia's Air Power: Capabilities and Structure* (Wien: Harpia Publishing, 2019)

Collins, L., 'In 2014, the "decrepit" Ukrainian army hit the refresh button. Eight years later, it's paying off', *The Conversation* (online), 8 March 2022

Cooper, T., *Moscow's Game of Poker: Russian Military Intervention in Syria, 2015–2017* (Warwick: Helion and Company, 2018)

Darczewska, J., *Rosgvardiya; A Special-Purpose Force* (Warsaw: OSW, Point of View 78, May 2020)

Defense Intelligence Agency, *Russia Military Power; Building a Military to support Great Power Aspirations* (DIA, 2017)

Delanoe, I., *Russia's Black Sea Fleet: Toward a Multiregional Force* (Arlington: CNA, 2019)

Demonque, C., 'La Garde nationale de Russie (Rosgvardia): Dernier rempart de Vladimir Poutine', *Défense & Sécurité Internationale*, No 159, May–June 2022

Dorfman, Z., 'Secret CIA training program in Ukraine helped Kyiv prepare for Russian Invasion', Yahoo News (online), 16 March 2022

Elfving, J., *An Assessment of the Russian Airborne Troops and their Role on Tomorrow's Battlefield* (Washington DC: The Jamestown Foundation, 2021)

Facon, I., *La nouvelle armée russe* (Paris: L'Observatoire franco-russe, 2021)

Fiore, N. J., 'Defeating the Russian Battalion Tactical Group', *Armour*, No. CXXVIII, Spring 2017

Fox, A. C., 'Cyborgs at Little Stalingrad: A Brief History of the Battles of the Donetsk Airport 26 May 2014 to 21 January 2015', *Land Warfare Paper*, No. 125, May 2019

Galeotti, M., 'Spetsnaz: Operational Intelligence, Political Warfare, and Battlefield Role', *Marshall Center Security Insight*, no. 46, Febuary 2020

Galeotti, M., 'Russian Airborne Forces re-tool for expanded Role', *Jane's* (online), 25 October 2021

Garamone, J., 'Ukraine-California Ties Show Worth of National Guard Program', *DoD News* (online), 18 March 2022

Goya, M., 'Offensives éclairs dans le Donbass- août 2014/janvier 2015', *La voix de l'épée* (online), 21 February 2022

Grant, G., 'Seven Years of Deadlock: Why Ukraine's Military Reforms Have Gone Nowhere, and How the US Should Respond', *The Jamestown Foundation*, 16 July 2021

Grau, L. W. & Bartles, C. K., *The Russian Way of War; Force Structure, Tactics, and Modernization of the Russian Ground Forces* (Fort Leavenworth: Foreign Military Studies Office, 2017)

Grau, L. W. & Bartles, C. K., 'Getting to Know the Russian Battalion Tactical Group', *The Royal United Services Institute* (online), 14 April 2022

Gressel, G., 'Waves of Ambition: Russia's Military Build-up in Crimea and the Black Sea' (European Council on Foreign Relations, 2021)

Harris, Catherine, Kagan Frederick W., *Russia's Military Posture: Ground Forces order of battle* (Washington: Institute for the Study of War, 2018)

Headquarters, Department of the Army, *Field Manual 100-2-3; The Soviet Army, Troops, Organization and Equipment* (Washington DC: Department of the Army, 1991)

Henrotin, Joseph, Guerre en Ukraine: le rôle de l'artillerie, in *Défense & Sécurité Internationale* (Hors-Série) no 72, June-July 2020

Henrotin, Joseph, L'armée ukrainienne: Une réforme impossible ?, in *Défense & Sécurité Internationale* no 157, January-February 2022

Holcomb, Franklin, *The order of Battle of the Ukrainian Armed Forces: A key component in European Security* (Washington: Institute for the Study of War, 2016)

Hunder Max, Government to create 26 Territorial Defense battalions, in *The Kyiv Independent*, 19 January 2022

Hunter, James, F-15 Eagle Driver On What It Is Like Flying Against Ukraine's Fighter Pilots, in *The Drive* (online), 29 March 2022

Janes, Ukraine conflict, Equipment profile, *Janes* (on line), 28 February 2022

Karber, Phillip A., *Lessons learned from the Russo-Ukrainian War (Draft)*, The Potomac Foundation, 29 September 2015

Karber, Phillip A., Thibeault, Josuah, Russia's New Generation Warfare, in *Army*, June 2016

Kossov, Igor, Ukraine's new military branch: Citizens protecting their neighborhood, in *Politico*, 13 February 2022

Lapaiev Yuri, Reforming Territorial Defense in Ukraine: Danger in Delay, in *Eurasia Daily Monitor* Volume 18, Issue 30, 23 February 2021

Manash Pratim, Boruah & Prathamesh, Karl, Ukrainian Navy: A force in distress, Janes (online), 15 February 2022

Ministry of Defence of Ukraine, *White Book 2013*; The Armed Forces of Ukraine (Kyiv, 2014)

Ministry of Defence of Ukraine, *White Book 2014*; The Armed Forces of Ukraine (Kyiv, 2015)

Ministry of Defence of Ukraine, *White Book 2015*; The Armed Forces of Ukraine (Kyiv, 2016)

Ministry of Defence of Ukraine, *White Book 2016*; The Armed Forces of Ukraine (Kyiv, 2017)

Ministry of Defence of Ukraine, *White Book 2017*; The Armed Forces of Ukraine (Kyiv, 2018)

Ministry of Defence of Ukraine, *White Book 2019–2020*; The Armed Forces of Ukraine (Kyiv, 2021)

Mladenov, A., 'Tough Days for Ukraine's military Helicopter Community', *Kiakaha Medias*, 23 August 2020

Muzyka, K., *Russian Forces in the Western Military District* (Arlington: CNA, 2021)

National Guard of Ukraine; *National Guard of Ukraine. Changes, development, achievements* (Documentary, July 2020)

Newdick, Thomas, Ukrainian MiG-29 Pilot's Front-Line Account Of The Air War Against Russia, *The Drive* (online), 1 April 2022

Ostensen, A. G. & Bukkvoll, T., *Russian Use of Private Military and Security Companies – the Implications for European and Norwegian Security* (Kjeller: The Norwegian Defence Research Establishment/FFI, 2018)

Ponomarenko, Illia, Who can and can't join Ukraine's Territorial Defense Force, in *The Kyiv Independent*, 7 January 2022

Pukhov, Ruslan, *The Tanks of August* (Moscow: Centre for Analysis of Strategies and Technologies, 2010)

Putiata, Dmytro, Karbivnychyi, Andrii , Rudyka, Vasyl, *Ukraine Armed Forces on the Eve of the Conflict* in mil.in.ua (online) 12 March 2020

Rector, Alexander, N.Y Army Guard Soldiers mentor and learn in Ukraine, *National Guard* (online) 22 June 2018

Ripley, Tim, *Operation Aleppo; Russia's War in Syria* (Lancaster: Telic-Herrick Publications, 2018)

Roblin, Sebastian, Meet the BTR-4: Watch Ukraine's "Bucephalus" Blast Russian Armored Vehicles, *1945* (online), 19 March 2022

Sanders, Deborah, "Rebuilding the Ukrainian Navy" in *Naval War College Review*, Volume 70, Number 4, 2017

Singh, Mandeep, The First Casualty: Suppression of Ukraine's Air Defences, *Northlines* (online), 26 February 2022

Stepanenko, Kateryna, Frederick W. Kagan, and Brian Babcock-Lumish, Explainer on Russian Conscription, Reserve, and Mobilization, *Institute for the Study War & The Critical Threats Project 2022* (online), 5 March 2022

Sukhankin, Sergey, and Hurska Alla, The Ukrainian Navy in the Black and Azov Seas after 2014: losses, achievements, prospects. *Policy Brief*, Special Edition.

US Army Training and Doctrine Command, *Russia Military; Quick Reference Guide* (TRADOC, 2020)

Trendafilovski, Vladimir, Ukrainian Naval Aviation Update, KeyMilitary (online), 16 January 2020

Welt, Cory, Russia's Use of Force Against the Ukrainian Navy, *CRS INSIGHT*, December 3, 2018

Wilk, Andrzej, *OSW Studies no 66: The best army Ukraine has ever had; Changes in Ukraine's armed forces since the Russian aggression* (Warsaw: Centre for Eastern Studies, 2017)

White, Andrew, Ukraine conflict: Ukrainian special operations forces in focus, *Janes* (online), 4 March 2022

Zagorodnyuk, Andriy, Alina Frolova, Hans Petter Midtunn & Oleksii Pavliuchyk, Is Ukraine's reformed military ready to repel a new Russian Invasion? *The Atlantic Council* (online), 23 December 2021

NOTES

Chapter 1

1. 'Putin shares the opinion that if there is a 'Revolution' in Ukraine, then there is a new state on its territory' (in Ukrainian), *Mirror Weekly*, 4 March 2014.
2. These events will be thoroughly covered in forthcoming volumes of this mini-series.
3. Galeotti (2019) pp. 54–56, Grant et al; Wilk pp. 10–11, 17–18, 25, *White Book* 2013, p. 67.
4. 'Ukraine's Army is back', *Unian Information Agency*, 28 February 2018.
5. Notably, by issuing of refurbished MT-12 Rapira 100mm anti-tank guns to the anti-tank 'divisions' of every brigade. Although outdated, these proved highly effective during the fighting in Donbas.
6. Organisation-wise, ZSU mechanised brigades are very similar to motor rifle regiments of the VSRF.
7. Dorfman, Zagorodnyuk & Ali, Garamone, Collins, Rector, Wilk, pp. 22–24.
8. Including Land Forces, Naval Infantry and Air Assault brigades.
9. *White Book 2013*; pp. 66, 70, *White Book 2014*; pp. 20, 30, 74; *White Book 2015*; pp. 10, 21, 24–26, 97–98; *White Book 2016*; pp. 11, 29, 30, 107–109; *White Book 2017*; pp. 14, 47, 68, 148–49, *White Book 2019–2020*; pp. 76, 83–84; Wilk, p. 16; Galeotti (2019) pp. 45–46; interview with Siarhei Franchuk, 10 March 2022.
10. Vladimir Shchetinin, quoted by Grant.
11. Wilk, pp. 28–30; Galeotti (2019), pp. 47–48; Grant; Ukroboronprom website. Content of successive White Books published by the Ministry of Defence (MOD) attest to the massive scale of the Ukrainian re-armament program, but much of the data they provide is contradictory, at other times unclear, and it remains unclear exactly how many of what major weapons systems had been overhauled and returned to service, and how many newly acquired. The above-listed numbers are thus within realms of 'best estimates'.
12. SIPRI Arms Transfers Database (as of 16 March 2022); Gotkowska, Justyna & Ali, 'NATO member states on arms deliveries to Ukraine', *OSW Commentary* No 423, 3 February 2022; Mitzer, Stijn, 'Keeping The Peace – Bayraktar TB2s Over Ukraine', *Oryx blog*, 7 January 2022.
13. Data provided in this sub-chapter and Appendix I is drawn from a wide range of Ukrainian sources, including official publications and the *White Book 2019–2021*, pp. 173–175, *MilitaryLand.net* website; Henrotin (2022); Siarhei Franchuk, interview, March 2022; White et al, pp. 21, 35–36; and Holcomb, pp. 11-15. For easier oversight, all units belonging to different commands of the Land Forces and the National Guard had been listed in Appendix I. This does not necessarily reflect their actual assignment as of February–March 2022.
14. Fontanellaz, Guerre en Ukraine, 'Orties: l'App disruptive au service du dieu de la guerre', LinkedIn.com, 21 May 2022.
15. Axe, 12 February 2022; Mladenov, 23 August 2020, *White Book 2019–2020*, p. 182.
16. Lapaiev, Kossov, Ponomarenko, Hunder, Grant, and interview with Siarhei Franchuk, 10 March 2022.
17. *National Guard of Ukraine. Changes, development, achievements*, July 2020, FIEP, *the National Guard of Ukraine*; MilitaryLand, consulted 19 March 2022.
18. 'Juice' (MiG-29 pilot), interview with Newdick, 1 April 2022.
19. Hunter, 29 March 2022.
20. *White Book* 2013, pp. 12, 71; *White Book* 2014. p. 78; *White Book* 2016, p. 108; *White Book* 2017, pp. 50, 148; *White Book* 2019–2020, pp. 182–183; Hunter, James, 29 March 2022; Newdick, 1 April 2022.
21. Axe, David, 27 January 2022; Boruah Manash Pratim & Karl Prathamesh, 15 February 2022; *Janes* (online), 28 February 2022; Sukhankin Sergey & Alla Hurska; Deborah Sanders, Cory Welt.
22. Trendafilovski, 16 January 2020.

Chapter 2

1. The German word *Aktiengesellschaft* defines a corporation limited by share ownership (i.e. one owned by its shareholders), and traded on a stock market. Considering the organisation and methods of operation of the regime of Vladimir Vladimirovich Putin in the Russian Federation, the authors find that this is the most suitable description.

2   The two conventions in question are the Vienna Convention on Succession of States in Respect of Treaties, from 1978, and the Vienna Convention on Succession of States in Respect of State Property, Archives, and Debts, of 1983.
3   The only former state of the USSR not recognising the exclusive Russian claims to succession of the Soviet Union was Ukraine: ever since 1991, Kyiv continued to pursue claims against the Russian Federation in foreign courts, seeking to recover its share of the foreign property that was formerly owned by the USSR.
4   Facon, pp. 11, 14–18, 23–26, 37, 39.
5   Beehner et al (2018), pp. 41–43, Pukov, pp. 18, 20, 40–41, 45, 49, 57, 75, 96, 113, 130–135, 142–143.
6   Facon, p. 35; Beehner et al (2018), pp. 49–50; Pukhov pp. 40, 136, 142.
7   Facon pp. 37, 38, 39, 49, Galeotti (2017), pp. 20–21, 25–34, 41, 49, Grau (2017), pp. 10, 27–29, 31, Stepanenko & Ali.
8   Facon p. 50–51, 54.
9   Fiore, Grau (2017) pp. 36–38, Grau (2022).
10 Based on Fox (2019) pp. 7–11, Galeotti (2019) pp. 11, 14, 16–17, 31–35. Goya, 21 February 2022, Karber (2015), Karber and Thibeault (2016), Henrotin (2020).
11 For details on the Russian military intervention in Syria, see Cooper, *Moscow's Game of Poker*.
12 Fore a more favourable assessment of the VSRF's capabilities demonstrated in Syria, see Ripley, pp. 197–1982 and 197.
13 Grau et al, p. 11.
14 Based on Fox (2019) pp. 7–11; Galeotti (2019), pp. 11, 14, 16–17, 31–35; Goya, 21 February 2022; Karber (2015); Karber and Thibeault (2016); Henrotin (2020).
15 Unless stated otherwise, based on Pavel Luzin, 'The Russian Army in 2023', *ridl.io*, 18 January 2023.
16 All brigades bore the official designation 'independent/separate', thus designating them as not part of divisions; this is omitted from all such designations in this book for reasons of space.
17 An abbreviation for *spetsialnovo naznacheniya*, or 'special purpose', Spetsnaz has a wide range of meanings in Russian but has come to be used colloquially to refer to special forces.
18 Muzyka, pp. 26, 30–32; Elfving, pp. 9–13, 17–20, 27; Galeotti (2017), pp. 49–51; Galeotti (2021); Grau (2017), pp. 32, 359–360; DIA (2017) p. 55.
19 Galleotti (2017), pp. 45–46, 51, 54; Grau (2017); pp. 32, 279–280, 362–363; Muzyka, p. 49; DIA (2017), pp. 56, 71.
20 Circular Error Probable (or CEP) is the distance from the target within which 50 percent of weapons could be expected to land, thus 50 percent of Iskander missiles could be expected to land within 20–30 metres of the aiming point.
21 Muzyka, pp. 10, 13, 23; Grau (2017), p. 31, 32, 34, 35, 100, 101, 209–211, 224, 264; Harris and Kagan, pp. 52–53; Galeotti (2017) p. 28; TRADOC (2020); DIA (2017) pp. 50–51, 53–54. Notably, the VSRF deployed about a dozen TOS-1/TOS-1A multiple rocket launcher systems to Ukraine in 2022. However, these short ranged tactical 220mm rocket systems, firing thermobaric warheads, were not assigned to the army's artillery units, but to the Russian NBC Protection Troops. This is why the weapon had no designation based on the designation system of the Main Missile and Artillery Directorate of the Ministry of Defence (so-called GRAU-designation).
22 Despite quite a lot of related reporting in the West of 2015–2017, as of the first half of 2022, there was no evidence that the UTCS was in service with MBT and IFV crews of the VSRF. Furthermore, while the Russian armed forces did have an ATMS at strategic and operational levels – and operated their air defences with the help of ATMS – they were yet to introduce a link between these and the UTCS and the ATMS used at higher command levels.
23 Unless stated otherwise, based on Butowski pp. 118,124; Grau (2017), pp. 25–26; Demonque et al (2020), pp. 7–8, 14–15, 22, 33, 39–40, 44, 54–57.
24 'Roughly speaking, we started the War: How sending Wagner PMC to the Front helped Prigozhin to improve Relations with Putin, and what is Sobyaninsky Regiment' (in Russian), *Meduza.io*, 13 July 2022.
25 Unless stated otherwise, based on Butowski (2019) and Cooper (2018). Aerial warfare over Ukraine in 2022 will be covered in much more detail in another book in this sub-series.
26 Gressel 2021, pp. 6, 10, Delanoe, pp. 1, 3–7, 11, 14, 16–17, 22, 24: Pukhov, p. 66; DIA (2017), pp. 67–69, 83.
27 Grau (2017), p. 143.
28 Based on Grau (2017) pp. 16, 25, 46–47, 51, 54–58, 143, 212, 224, 232–235, 239, 265, 289, 329–330.

Chapter 3

Chapter 4

1   Указ Президента Российской Федерации от 21.02.2022 № 71 "О признании Донецкой Народной Республики"; http://publication.pravo.gov.ru/Document/View/0001202202220002; Обращение Президента Российской Федерации, 21 February 2022, http://kremlin.ru/events/president/news/67828; Путин: Россия признала ДНР и ЛНР в границах Донецкой и Луганской областей, BBC News website, 22 February 2022, https://www.bbc.com/russian/news-60483790.
2   Volodymyr Zolkin, 'Aiming in the Residential Quarters of Mariinka', YouTube, 8 July 2022.
3   'Ukraine munitions blasts prompt mass Evacuations', BBC News, 23 March 2017; 'NATO Envoys arrive in Balaklia to assist in humanitarian demining', UNIAN, 25 March 2017; 'Ammo Depot explosions in Kharkiv region's Balaklia stop on Thursday afternoon', UNIAN, 3 May 2018; 'Ukraine's exploding Munition Depots give Ammunition to Security Concerns', *Radio Free Europe*, 6 October 2017.
4   Andrew S Bowen, 'Russian Military Buildup Along the Ukrainian Border', Congressional Research Service, 7 February 2022, Rochan Consulting, 'Tracking Russian Deployments near Ukraine – Autumn–Winter 2021–22', 15 November 2021. For details on Operation Danube, see Francois, *Operation Danube*, Europe@War.
5   Andrew S Bowen, 'Russian Military Buildup Along the Ukrainian Border', Congressional Research Service, 7 February 2022, Rochan Consulting, 'Tracking Russian Deployments near Ukraine – Autumn–Winter 2021–22', 15 November 2021; Dan Sabbagh, 'Putin involved in War "at level of Colonel or Brigadier", say Western Sources', *The Guardian*, 16 May 2022.
6   Andrew S Bowen, 'Russian Military Buildup Along the Ukrainian Border', Congressional Research Service, 7 February 2022, Rochan Consulting, 'Tracking Russian Deployments near Ukraine – Autumn–Winter 2021–22', 15 November 2021.
7   Garamon.
8   Slava (veteran NCO of the ZSU), interview, 20 February 2022; Dan Rice, 'The Untold Story of the Battle for Kyiv', *Small Wars Journal* (online), 31 May 2022; Paul Sonne, Isabelle Khurshudyan, Serhiy Morgunov, Kostiantyn Khudov, 'Battle for Kyiv: Ukrainian Valor, Russian Blunders combined to save the Capital', *WP*, 24 August 2022.

Chapter 5

1. Robert Person, Michael McFaul, 'What Putin fears most', *Journal of Democracy*, Vol. 33/Issue 2, April 2022; Samuel Ramani, 'Russia and the UAE: An Ideational Partnership', *Middle East Policy*, 25 April 2020; Maria Tsvetkova, 'How Russia allowed homegrown Radicals to go and fight in Syria', Reuters, 13 May 2016; Stuart Ramsay, 'IS Files reveal Assad's Deal with Militants', Sky News, 2 May 2016; Sabra Ayres, 'Thousands of Russians joined Islamic State and brought their Children. Now Relatives are trying to bring them Home', *Los Angeles Times*, 26 October 2017; Hassan Hassan, 'Insurgents Again: the Islamic State's calculated Reversion to Attrition in the Syria-Iraq Border Region and beyond', *Combating Terrorism Center at West Point*, Volume 10, Issue 11, December 2017; for a detailed reconstruction of the Iranian and then the Russian military interventions in Syria, see Cooper, *Syrian Conflagration* & Cooper, *Moscow's Game of Poker* (details in Bibliography).
2. 'Operation Z: The Death Throes of an Imperial Delusion', RUSI, Special Report, 22 April 2022, p. 2.
3. Joe Tidy, 'Ukrainian power grid "lucky" to withstand Russian cyber-attack', *BBC*, 12 April 2022.
4. 'Operation Z: The Death Throes of an Imperial Delusion', RUSI, Special Report, 22 April 2022, p. 2.
5. Unless stated otherwise, the following reconstruction of the fighting north-west of Kyiv between 24 and 28 February is based on cross-examination of dozens of reports in the mainstream and social media, including – for example – Dan Rice, 'The untold Story of the Battle for Kyiv', *Small Wars Journal* (online), 31 May 2022 – and a review of videos released on YouTube, including 'The Hostomel Landing Analysis', 26 May 2022; 'Russian Ka-52 Emergency Landing during Combat Sortie at Hostomel Airport', 19 March 2022; 'Helmet Cam captured Russian Air Assault Troops First Capture of Hostomel Airport', 12 March 2022; Russian 'Special Military Operation' in Ukraine, 25 March 2022 and 'Survivor: Russian VDV Airborne Soldier talks about their initial Invasion of Hostomel Airport', 21 April 2022.
6. Paul Sonne, Isabelle Khurshudyan, Serhiy Morgunov, Kostiantyn Khudov, 'Battle for Kyiv: Ukrainian Valor, Russian Blunders combined to save the Capital', *The Washington Post* (WP), 24 August 2022.
7. Notably, members of the 4th Rapid Intervention Brigade, NG, reported the arrival of 34 Russian helicopters at Antonov IAP, and to have shot down three of these (see 'Video shows Helicopters flying towards Gostomel Airfield in Ukraine', *WP*, 24 February 2022). If the Russian formation originally included a total of 40 helicopters, this might be a cross-confirmation of the loss of up to six, and heavy damage of at least three Ka-52s, Mi-8s and Mi-24s – to PSU interceptors and ZSU MANPADs.
8. Sonne et al, 'Battle for Kyiv…', *WP*, 24 August 2022.
9. Zolkin, 'Survivor…', *YouTube*; 21 April 2022; Ukrainian Military TV, 'Zeus: A Man who beat Russians hard in Hostomel', YoOTube, 15 August 2022; James Marson, 'The Ragtag Army that won the Battle of Kyiv and saved Ukraine', *WSJ*, 20 September 2022.
10. Julian Duplain, 'Russians twice targeted Zelensky compound with attacks, Ukraine says', *Washington Post*, 29 April 2022; Sonne et al, 'Battle for Kyiv…', *WP*, 24 August 2022.
11. 'The Destruction of a Convoy of Chechen Special Forces near Hostomel on Feb. 26 officially confirmed by the President's Office', *Kyiv Independent*, 27 February 2022 & Slava (veteran NCO of the ZSU), interview, 10 March 2022.
12. James Marson, 'The Ragtag Army…', *WSJ*, 20 September 2022.
13. Zolkin, 'Survivor…', YouTube, 21 April 2022.
14. 'How this War began: Interview with General Krivonos by Mark Solonin' (in Ukrainian), *YouTube.com*, 29 July 2022.
15. Based on media reports (for example; *Kyiv Independent, Washington Examiner, CNN* etc.) by mayor of Vasylkiv, Natalya Balasinovich, and Kryvonos's interview with Mark Solonin. Zaluzhny claimed an Il-76 shot down over Vasylkiv via his Telegram account early on 26 February, and this claim was repeated by the Associated Press. The Pentagon 'confirmed' the downing of two Il-76s. That said, as of summer 2022, the Ukrainians have not provided any kind of evidence for any of these intercepts or at least for a major engagement with the VDV on the ground.

Chapter 6

1. Andrew Milburn, 'They own the long Clock: How the Russian military is starting to adapt in Ukraine', Taskandpurpose.com, 21 March 2022; Andrew Milburn, 'Russia's War in Ukraine is far from over', Taskandpurpose.com, 21 March 2022; Andrew Milburn, Interview, Taskandpurpose.com, 25 March 2022; 'Operation Z: The Death Throes of an Imperial Delusion', RUSI, Special Report, 22 April 2022, p. 4.
2. Isobel Koshiw, 'How Sumy's Residents kept Russian Forces out of their City', *The Guardian*, 2 January 2023.
3. 'Awaiting an Order: Battalion Commander on Kharkiv Counteroffensive, Possibility of War in Russia' (in Ukrainian), *Hromadske*, 23 May 2022.
4. Cross-examination of reports by Stariy & Butusov, *25 Russian Military Vehicles destroyed near Stariy Saltiv*, 9 May 2022.
5. 'Awaiting an Order: Battalion Commander on Kharkiv Counteroffensive, Possibility of War in Russia' (in Ukrainian), *Hromadske*, 23 May 2022.

Chapter 7

1. В "ДНР" и "ЛНР" объявлена всеобщая мобилизация, DW, 19 February 2022; 'Глава ЛНР Пасечник подписал указ о всеобщей мобилизации в республике', RT, 19 February 2022, 'В ДНР и ЛНР военные силой забирают жителей на войну', URA.ua, 21 February 2022, 'Росія почала військову окупацію частини Донбасу: з'явилось відео входження колони техніки', TSN, 21 February 2022.
2. 'В ЛНР заявили, что у республики не будет легкой операции в Донбассе', Ria Novosti, 24 February 2022.
3. 'Оккупанты "ЛНР" объявили о начале штурма прифронтового Счастья (видео)', Focus.ua, 24 February 2022; '«Счастье не дадим потерять стране». Как жители города в Луганской области выживают во время обострения на фронте, Hromadske.ua, 24 February 2022.
4. 'ВСУ отбили атаку на прифронтовое Счастье, город остается под контролем Украины', Focus.ua, 24 February 2022, 'Плацдарменное положение: Луганская республика начала решающие бои', Izvestia, 28 February 2022. In early March 2022, the government of Ukraine opened a case for treason against the head of the Stanytssia Luhanska civil-military administration and his two deputies, allegedly for switching sides and providing intelligence and support to the LPR and Russian forces (see: 'Держзрада керівників селищної військово-цивільної адміністрації на Луганщині – розпочато розслідування', Ukrainian Prosecutor's Office website, 2 March 2022).
5. Ukrainian Military TV, 'AFU destroyed 2 enemy tanks and 1 IFV near Triokhizbenka', YouTube, 25 February 2022; 'Город Счастье и семь поселков освобождены в ЛНР', Don24.ru, 28 February 2022.

6   'Кольцевая линия: войска республик Донбасса и России блокировали Мариуполь', Izvestia, 2 March 2022; Теперь работаем вместе, 'Войска ЛНР и армия России вышли навстречу друг другу в Донбассе', YouTube, 4 March 2022.
7   This is a common community name in Donbas, for reference this is the Petrivske listed in the Ukrainian gazetteer as being located at 37.83651 47.63066. 'Басурин заявил, что силы ДНР будут освобождать территорию области', RIA Novosti, 24 February 2022; 'Луганское Счастье: как в ЛНР налаживают жизнь под залпы артиллерии', Izvestia, 5 March 2022.
8   'Українські військові поблизу Волновахи збили російський винищувач-бомбардувальник, Slovo I Dilo, 3 March 2022; 'Освобождение Мариуполя: морпехи Новороссии против морпехов Украинского Государства', 9111.ru, 24 March 2022; 'В Волновахе уничтожен командир батальона "Спарта" из ДНР', Dnepr Express, 6 March 2022.
9   'Бронеавтомобили "Варта" на вооружении народной милиции ДНР', VK website, 12 March 2022

Chapter 8

1   'The Heroes of the Moment in Time: Blew up Bridge together with Himself', GenStab-U, 25 February 2022.
2   Ukrainian Military TV, 'Ihor Skybiuk, about the first Days of War and Defending Voznesensk', 16 July 2022; 'Поранені майже не виживають: у розвідці назвали кількість втрат серед мобілізованих на Донбасі', Kanal 24, 19 May 2022; UK Ministry of Defence, 'Latest Defence Intelligence update on the situation in Ukraine – 22 June 2022'
3   'A Ukrainian Town deals Russia one of the War's most decisive Routs'. WSJ, 16 March 2022; Sravasti Dasgupta, 'Ukrainian Soldiers and Volunteers defeated larger Russian force in strategically important Town', *The Independent*, 17 March 2022; 'Paratroopers from the Lviv Region repulsed the enemy attack on in the Battle for Voznesensk', 26 March 2022; 'Film shows Battle for Voznesensk, which kept Russians from reaching Odesa', 15 April 2022; Ukrainian Military TV, 'Ihor Skybiuk, about the first Days of War and Defending Vozunesenks', 16 July 2022.

Appendix III

1   Unless stated otherwise, based on Butowski.

ABOUT THE AUTHORS

Tom Cooper is an aerial warfare analyst and historian from Austria. While mostly specialising in research and publishing on small, little-known air forces and conflicts, about which he has collected extensive archives, his coverage of the war in Syria eventually prompted him into researching the Russian air force – and thus the War in Ukraine. Since 2017, Cooper has worked as the editor of the six @War book series.

Adrien Fontanellaz, from Switzerland, is a military history researcher and author. He developed a passion for military history at an early age and has progressively narrowed his studies to modern-day conflicts. He is a member of the Scientific Committee of the Pully-based Centre d'Histoire et de Prospective Militaires (Military History and Prospectives Centre), and regularly contributes for the *Revue Militaire Suisse* and various French military history magazines.

Edward Crowther lived and worked in Donetsk, the capital of the self-declared 'Donetsk People's Republic' in eastern Ukraine for two and half years from 2016 to early 2019. He holds an MSc and BSc. This is his second work for Helion.

Milos Sipos is a Slovakian military historian. While pursuing a career in law he has collected extensive documentation on interconnected political, industrial, and human resources and military-related affairs in Iran, Iraq, Syria, and Russia. His core interest is a systematic approach to studies of their deep impacts upon combat efficiency and the general performance of different armed forces. After more than 10 years of related work on the ACIG.info forum, he has co-authored numerous books published in Helion's @War series.